THINKING THROUGH SOURCES

for

Ways of the World

A Brief Global History

VOLUME 1: THROUGH THE FIFTEENTH CENTURY

ROBERT W. STRAYER

The College at Brockport: State University of New York

ERIC W. NELSON

Missouri State University

THIRD EDITION

bedford/st.martin's
Macmillan Learning
Boston | New York

For Evelyn Rhiannon with Love

For Bedford/St. Martin's

*Vice President, Editorial, Macmillan Learning
Humanities:* Edwin Hill
Publisher for History: Michael Rosenberg
Acquiring Editor for History: Laura Arcari
Director of Development for History: Jane Knetzger
Senior Developmental Editor: Leah R. Strauss
Senior Production Editor: Christina M. Horn
Assistant Production Editor: Erica Zhang
Production Manager: Joe Ford
Executive Marketing Manager: Sandra McGuire
Copy Editor: Jennifer Brett Greenstein
Photo Researcher: Bruce Carson
Director of Rights and Permissions: Hilary Newman
Senior Art Director: Anna Palchik

Text Design: Joyce Weston
Cover Design: William Boardman
Cover Photos: top, Moai (megalithic
anthropomorphic statues) near Rano Raraku
Volcano, Rapa Nui National Park (Unesco
World Heritage List, 1995), Easter Island, Chile,
Polynesian Civilization/De Agostini Picture
Library/W. Buss/Bridgeman Images; bottom,
Kublai Khan (1214–94) Hunting, Yuan dynasty
(ink & colour on silk) (detail), Liu Kuan-tao
(fl. 1270–1300) (attr. to)/National Palace
Museum, Taipei, Taiwan/Bridgeman Images
Composition: Jouve
Printing and Binding: RR Donnelley

Manufactured in the United States of America.

1   0   9   8   7
f   e   d

For information, write: Bedford/St. Martin's, 75 Arlington Street, Boston, MA 02116
(617-399-4000)

ISBN 978-1-319-07464-7 (Volume 1)
ISBN 978-1-319-07465-4 (Volume 2)

THINKING THROUGH SOURCES

for

Ways of the World

A Brief Global History

Preface

Designed specifically to be used with all versions of *Ways of the World*, Third Edition, this document collection complements and extends each chapter of the parent textbook. As the title of the collection suggests, these document projects enable students to **"think through sources"** and thus begin to understand the craft of historians as well as their conclusions. They explore in greater depth a central theme from each chapter, and they integrate both documentary and visual sources. Each source includes a brief headnote that provides context for the source and several questions to consider, and the chapter ends with a series of probing essay questions appropriate for in-class discussion and writing assignments.

In addition to this print volume, we are delighted to offer the **Thinking through Sources document projects** in LaunchPad, Bedford's learning platform. In LaunchPad, these features are surrounded by a distinctive and sophisticated pedagogy of auto-graded exercises. Featuring immediate substantive feedback for each rejoinder, these exercises help students learn even when they select the wrong answer. These unique exercises guide students in assessing their understanding of the sources, in organizing those sources for use in an essay, and in drawing useful conclusions from them. In this interactive learning environment, students will enhance their ability to build arguments and to practice historical reasoning.

More specifically, a short **quiz after each source** offers students the opportunity to check their understanding of materials that often derive from quite distant times and places. Some questions focus on audience, purpose, point of view, limitations, or context, while others challenge students to draw conclusions about the source or to compare one source with another. Immediate substantive feedback for each rejoinder and the opportunity to try again create an active learning environment where students are rewarded for reaching the correct answer through their own process of exploration.

Two activities at the end of each Thinking through Sources exercise ask students to make supportable inferences and draw appropriate conclusions from sources with reference to a **Guiding Question**. In the **Organize the Evidence activity**, students identify which sources provide evidence for a topic that would potentially compose part of an answer to the guiding question. In the **Draw Conclusions from the Evidence activity**, students assess whether a specific piece of evidence drawn from the sources supports or challenges a conclusion related to the guiding question. Collectively these assignments create an active learning environment where reading with a purpose is reinforced by immediate feedback and support. The guiding question provides a foundation for in-class activities or a summative writing assignment.

To learn more about the benefits of LaunchPad and the different versions of *Ways of the World* to package with LaunchPad, visit **macmillanhighered.com /strayersources/catalog**.

Acknowledgments

We extend our thanks to acquiring editor Laura Arcari, senior development editor Leah Strauss, senior production editor Christina Horn, and assistant production editor Erica Zhang of Bedford/St. Martin's.

Robert Strayer, La Selva Beach, California, Winter 2016
Eric Nelson, Springfield, Missouri, Winter 2016

Contents

8 The Making of Japanese Civilization   93

9 Voices of Islam   106

10 The Crusades as Cultural Encounter   120

11 Living and Dying during the Black Death   134

12 Early Encounters; First Impressions   147

THINKING THROUGH SOURCES

for

Ways of the World

A Brief Global History

CHAPTER 1

THINKING THROUGH SOURCES

History before Writing:
How Do We Know?

Written records have long been the chief source of data for historians seeking to reconstruct the past. But writing is a quite recent innovation in the long journey of humankind, emerging with the advent of the first civilizations only about 5,000 years ago. This absence of written records for earlier phases of human history is one of the reasons many world historians have neglected or avoided the Paleolithic and Neolithic eras.

And yet, all manner of techniques for probing the more distant past have evolved over the last century or so. An emerging field known as genetic anthropology uses DNA analysis to trace the movement of people across the planet. Linking genetic evidence with fossil remains, scholars have reached a general consensus that sub-Saharan Africa was the original home of our species, *Homo sapiens*. Historical linguistics, rooted in the changes that languages undergo, has also aided in tracking human movement and defining the character of particular cultures by analyzing their vocabularies. Our understanding of the widespread cultures of Indo-European and African Bantu-speaking peoples derives largely from such linguistic analysis. Anthropologists studying modern gathering and hunting societies have also shed light on the lives of our distant ancestors, while archeologists have contributed much to our grasp of the unwritten past through their study of human fossil remains, tools, pottery, buildings, art, and more. This collection of sources explores work by specialists in these final two fields to explore how we know about early human societies.

Source 1.1
A Gathering and Hunting Woman in the Twentieth Century

A somewhat controversial technique for doing history before writing lies in analogies with more recent nonliterate peoples. In the twentieth century, anthropologists and other scholars descended on the few remaining gathering and hunting peoples, studying their cultures and collecting their stories, myths, and oral traditions. For good reasons, historians are often skeptical about the usefulness of such material for understanding the distant past of Paleolithic societies. Since all societies change over time, is it reasonable to think that contemporary gathering and hunting societies would resemble in any way their ancestors thousands of years ago? Furthermore, there is the problem of contamination. After all, gatherers and hunters in recent times have often mixed and mingled with agricultural societies, come under European colonial rule, or made contact with elements of modern civilization. Other scholars, particularly teachers, have embraced these materials, even while recognizing their limitations, for they provide at least a glimpse into ways of living and thinking that have almost completely vanished from the earth.

Source 1.1 allows you to make a judgment about the usefulness of this approach to history before writing by examining the work of the American anthropologist Marjorie Shostak. In 1971, she was conducting research among the San people of the Kalahari Desert on the border of Botswana and South Africa, where she became acquainted with a fifty-year-old woman named Nisa. Although Nisa had interacted with neighboring cattle-keeping people and with Europeans, she had lived most of her life "in the bush," fully participating in the gathering and hunting culture of her ancestors. Nisa proved willing to share with Shostak the intimate details of her life, including her memories of childhood, her several marriages, the birth of her children, her relationships with various lovers, and the deaths of loved ones. Those interviews became the basis for the remarkable book from which the following excerpts derive.

Question to consider as you examine the source:

■ How useful do you find Nisa's account for understanding the life of much earlier Paleolithic people? What evidence of contact with a wider world can you find in her story?

NISA

The Life and Words of a !Kung Woman: Life in the Bush

We are people who live in the bush, and who belong in the bush. We are not village people. I have no goats. I have no cattle. I am a person who owns nothing.

That's what people say I am: a poor person. . . . No donkey, either. I still carry things myself, in my kaross [an animal hide cloak] when I travel. . . .

We lived and lived, and as I kept growing, I started to carry my little brother around on my shoulders. My heart was happy then; I had grown to love him and carried him everywhere. I'd play with him for a while and whenever he would start to cry, I'd take him to Mother so he could nurse. Then I'd take him back with me and we'd play together again.

That was when Kumsa was little. But once he was older and started to talk and then to run around, that's when we were mean to each other and hit and fought all the time. . . .

We lived in the bush and my father set traps and killed steenbok and duiker and gemsbok and we lived, eating the animals and foods of the bush. We collected food, ground it in a mortar, and ate it. We also ate sweet nin berries and tsin beans. When I was growing up, there were no cows or goats. . . . I had never seen other peoples and didn't know anything other than life in the bush. . . .

Whenever my father killed an animal and I saw him coming home with meat draped over a stick, balanced on one shoulder — that's what made me happy. I'd cry out, "Mommy! Daddy's coming and he's bringing meat!" My heart would be happy when I greeted him, "Ho, ho, Daddy! We're going to eat meat!" Or honey. Sometimes he'd go out and come home with honey. I'd be sitting around with my mother and then see something coming from way out in the bush. I'd look hard. Then, "Oooh, Daddy found a beehive! Oh, I'm going to eat honey!" . . . And I'd thank him and call him wonderful names. . . .

When we were living in the bush, some people gave and others stinged. But there were always enough people around who shared, people who liked one another, who were happy living together, and who didn't fight. And even if one person did stinge, the other person would just get up and yell about it, whether it was meat or anything else, "What's doing this to you, making you not give us meat?"

When I was growing up, receiving food made my heart happy. There really wasn't anything, other than stingy people, that made me unhappy. I didn't like people who wouldn't give a little of what they had. . . .

It's the same today. Here I am, long since an adult, yet even now, if a person doesn't give something to me, I won't give anything to that person. . . .

Marriage

. . . The day of the wedding, everyone was there. All of Tashay's friends were sitting around, laughing and laughing. His younger brother said, "Tashay, you're too old. Get out of the way so I can marry her. Give her to me." . . . They were all sitting around, talking like that. They all wanted me.

I went to my mother's hut and sat there. I was wearing lots of beads and my hair was completely covered and full with ornaments. . . . That night there was another dance. We danced, and some people fell asleep and others kept dancing. . . .

The next day they started [to build the marriage hut]. There were lots of people there — Tashay's mother, my mother, and my aunt worked on the hut; everyone else sat around, talking. Late in the day, the young men went and brought Tashay to the finished hut. They set him down beside it and stayed there with him, sitting around the fire. . . .

They came and brought me back. Then they laid me down inside the hut. I cried and cried. People told me, "A man is not something that kills you; he is someone who marries you, who becomes like your father or your older brother. He kills animals and gives you things to eat."

I listened and was quiet. Later, we went to sleep. Tashay lay down beside the opening of the hut, near the fire, and I lay down inside; he thought I might try and run away again. He covered himself with a blanket and slept. . . .

We lived and lived, the two of us, together, and after a while I started to really like him and then, to love him. I had finally grown up and had learned how to love. I thought, "A man has sex with you. Yes, that's what a man does. I had thought that perhaps he didn't."

We lived on and I loved him and he loved me. I loved him the way a young adult knows how to love; I just loved him. Whenever he went away and I stayed behind, I'd miss him. I'd think, "Oh, when is my husband ever coming home? How come he's been gone so long?" I'd miss him and want him. When he'd come back my heart would be happy, "Eh, hey! My husband left and once again has come back."

I . . . gave myself to him, gave and gave. We lay with each other and my breasts were very large. I was becoming a woman.

Loss

It was while we were visiting in the Tswana village [of cattle-keeping people] and just after Kxau was born that Tashay died. . . . I lay there and thought, "Why did this happen? The two of us gave so much to each other and lived together so happily. Now I am alone, without a husband. I am already a widow. Why did God trick me and take my husband? God is stingy! He just takes them from you. God's heart is truly far from people." . . .

Then I was without my husband and my heart was miserable. Every night I missed him and every night I cried, "I am without the man I married." I thought, "Where will I see the food that will help my children grow? Who is going to help me raise this newborn? ~~My older brother and my younger brother are far away.~~ Who is going to help me now?"

In your heart, your child, your mother, and your father are all equal. When any one of them dies, your heart feels pain. When your child dies, you think, "How come this little thing I held beside me and watched all that she did, today has died and left me? She was the only child I had with me. . . . This God . . . his ways are foul! Why did he give me a little one and then take her away?" . . .

The death of your parents, husband, or children — they are equal in the amount of pain you feel when you lose them. But when they all die and you have no family left, then you really feel pain. There is no one to take care of you; you are completely alone. . . .

That's the way it is. God is the one who destroys. It isn't people who do it. It is God himself.

Lovers   *started narrating*

. . . Besa [Nisa's fourth husband] and I did argue a lot, usually about sex. . . . Every night Besa wanted me and every night he would make love to me. That Besa, something was wrong with his brain! . . . After a while, I realized I didn't like his ways. That's when I thought, "Perhaps I will leave him. Perhaps I'll find another man and see what he is like."

I didn't leave him, not for many years. But I did have lovers and so did he. . . . Because

affairs . . . is something that even people from long ago knew. Even my father's father's father's father knew. There have also always been fights where poison arrows are shot and people are killed because of that. Having affairs is one of the things God gave us. . . .

When you are a woman, you don't just sit still and do nothing — you have lovers. You don't just sit with the man of your hut, with just one man. One man can give you very little. One man gives you only one kind of food to eat. But when you have lovers, one brings you something and another brings you something else. One comes at night with meat, another with money, another with beads. Your husband also does things and gives them to you. But sitting with just one man? We don't do that. Does one man have enough thoughts for you?

A Healing Ritual

. . . N/um — the power to heal — is a very good thing. This is a medicine very much like your medicine because it is strong. As your medicine helps people, our n/um helps people. But to heal with n/um means knowing how to trance. Because, it is in trance that the healing power sitting inside the healer's body — the n/um — starts to work. Both men and women learn how to cure with it, but not everyone wants to. Trance-medicine really hurts! As you begin to trance, the n/um slowly heats inside you and pulls at you. It rises until it grabs your insides and takes your thoughts away. Your mind and your senses leave and you don't think clearly. Things become strange and start to change. You can't listen to people or understand what they say. You look at them and they suddenly become very tiny. You think, "What's happening? Is God doing this?" All that is inside you is the n/um; that is all you can feel.

You touch people, laying on hands, curing those you touch. When you finish, other people hold you and blow around your head and your face. Suddenly your senses go "Phah!" and come back to you. You think, "Eh hey, there are people here," and you see again as you usually do. . . .

N/um is powerful, but it is also very tricky. Sometimes it helps and sometimes it doesn't, because God doesn't always want a sick person to get better. . . . I was a young woman when my mother and her younger sister started to teach me about drum-medicine. There is a root that helps you learn to trance, which they dug for me. My mother put it in my little leather pouch and said, "Now you will start learning this, because you are a young woman already." She had me keep it in my pouch for a few days. Then one day, she took it and pounded it along with some bulbs and some beans and cooked them together. It had a horrible taste and made my mouth feel foul. I threw some of it up. If she hadn't pounded it with the other foods, my stomach would have been much more upset and I would have thrown it all up; then it wouldn't have done anything for me. I drank it a number of times and threw up again and again. Finally I started to tremble. People rubbed my body as I sat there, feeling the effect getting stronger and stronger. My body

shook harder and I started to cry. I cried while people touched me and helped me with what was happening to me.

Eventually, I learned how to break out of myself and trance. When the drum-medicine songs sounded, that's when I would start. Others would string beads and copper rings into my hair. As I began to trance, the women would say, "She's started to trance, now, so watch her carefully. Don't let her fall." They would take care of me, touching me and helping. If another woman was also in a trance, she laid on hands and helped me. They rubbed oil on my face and I stood there — a lovely young woman, trembling — until I was finished.

Source: From NISA: THE LIFE AND WORDS OF A !KUNG WOMAN by Marjorie Shostak. Copyright © 1981 by Marjorie Shostak. Used by permission of Harvard University Press.

Source 1.2
Lascaux Rock Art

Physical remains studied by archeologists and others provide yet another point of entry into the history of nonliterate peoples. Among these, creative artistic representation has been especially useful, for it is as old as humankind itself, long preceding the emergence of urban civilizations. The most ancient of these artistic traditions are the rock paintings that Paleolithic people created all across the world.

Paleolithic art is found in many places, but perhaps the most well-known Paleolithic rock art comes from the Lascaux caves in southern France, discovered by several teenage boys in 1940. Dating to around 17,000 years ago, the cave walls depict various kinds of animals: numerous horses, stags, and bison; seven felines; and a single bear, rhinoceros, and bird. But no reindeer are included, although they were the main source of meat for the artists. Abstract designs consisting of dots and lines accompany many of the paintings.

Scholars have debated endlessly what insights these remarkable images might provide into the mental world of Paleolithic Europeans. Were they examples of "totemic" thinking — the belief that particular groups of men and women were associated with, or descended from, particular animals? Did they represent "hunting magic" intended to enhance the success of these early hunters? Because many of the paintings were located deep within caves, were they perhaps part of religious or ritual practices or rites of passage?

Were they designed to pass on information to future generations? Were the abstract designs star charts, as one scholar has suggested? Or did these images represent the visions of shamans, as some have also suggested for the South African rock painting in Chapter 1 (page 10) of the main text. No one really knows.

But beyond their uncertain meaning as archeological evidence for Paleolithic life, modern humans have recognized the artistic value of the Lascaux paintings, appreciating their graceful lines, use of color, and distinctive sense of perspective and sometimes movement. Tradition has it that the great twentieth-century artist Pablo Picasso remarked after viewing the caves that "we have learned nothing in 12,000 years."[1] Furthermore, the art of the Lascaux caves was part of a very long artistic tradition in the region that adhered over many millennia to a set of aesthetic conventions. Thus it was a conservative tradition, linked to a long-established social order and very much unlike modern art, which generally challenges contemporary society.

Questions to consider as you examine the source:

■ No one knows for certain if the three figures in this image were painted at the same time. But if they were, it represents a very early narrative composition. How might you tell the story that the painting depicts? Is the man dead or wounded? What message would such a story convey?

■ What differences do you notice between the portrayal of the human figure and that of the animals?

Lascaux Rock Art

Caves of Lascaux, Dordogne, France/Bridgeman Images

One of the most dramatic and perplexing images from Lascaux, shown here, depicts a human male figure lying in front of a wounded and enraged bison, pierced with a broken spear and with its entrails hanging out. To the left is a rhinoceros, and beneath its tail are two rows of three dots.

Source 1.3
Female Figurine from Çatalhüyük

In seeking to understand the Neolithic age — occurring between the beginnings of settled agriculture and the rise of literate civilizations — historians confront much the same problem as do scholars of the preceding Paleolithic era. In the absence of writing, they must depend heavily on material remains such as art, artifacts, and architecture. In comparison with Paleolithic society, which gave rise to relatively simple art, the new economy generated by agriculture gave rise to many artistic innovations. Weaving and pottery making became major industries, offering new opportunities for creative expression. While animals continued to be a focus of Neolithic art, human figures became more prominent and were more realistically depicted than in the cave paintings and Venus figurines of the Paleolithic era. But observers — both expert and amateur — continue to debate the meaning of these representations with no consensus in sight.

Among Neolithic sites, few have generated more controversy than Çatalhüyük in modern Turkey, particularly about the role of women in the religious and social life of this early agricultural village. The first major dig at the site, undertaken by James Mellaart in the 1960s, uncovered a number of small female figurines, the most famous of which is shown here as Source 1.3. It dates to about 5000 B.C.E. and is some eight inches in height. The baked-clay figure depicts a seated female whose arms are resting on two lionesses or leopards. For Mellaart, this was evidence for an ancient and powerful cult of the "mother Goddess," an idea that other scholars have dismissed. Despite the controversy, some goddess devotees have come to view Çatalhüyük as a pilgrimage site.

Later archeological research, ongoing since 1993 under the leadership of Ian Hodder, has called some aspects of this "mother Goddess" interpretation into question. Hodder, for example, doubts the existence of an organized cult with an attached priesthood, as Mellaart theorized. Rather, Hodder noted that the image suggests "a close connection between ritual and daily functions." He added:

> I do not think that there was a separate religious elite. I think the religion was an integral part of daily life. It may be wrong to think of the Çatal art as religious or symbolic at all. It may be more that people thought that they had to paint, or make relief sculptures, in order to achieve certain practical ends (such as make the crops grow, or prevent children from dying).[2]

Furthermore, Hodder suggested that while women were certainly prominent in the symbolism of the village, there is little evidence for a "matriarchal society" in which women dominated. Rather, he wrote that "men and women had the same social status. There was a balance of power."[3]

Questions to consider as you examine the source:

■ Without trying to interpret this statue, how would you simply describe it?

■ What features of this statue might support Mellaart's view? Which support Hodder's interpretation?

Female Figurine from Çatalhüyük

Source 1.4
Otzi the Ice Man

Beyond the artistic products of people without writing, historians have also learned much from their burial sites. Analysis of human remains often discloses something about diet, nutrition, and disease, while variations in burial materials can provide indications of social status, technology, religion, and more. Among the more famous burials of the Neolithic era was that of Otzi the Ice Man, a forty-six-year-old man, about five feet five inches tall, whose body was discovered in 1991 frozen in a glacier high in the Italian Alps. Properly speaking, it was not a burial at all, for Otzi, named for the region in which he was found, died far from home about 5,300 years ago in this remote mountainous area, his body left to the elements, which miraculously preserved it for over five millennia.

In his midforties, Otzi was an old man for his time and place, no doubt full of aches and pains. The condition of his bones and evidence of frostbite suggest that he spent much of his life in steep, cold, mountainous terrain. Some fifty-seven tattoos, made by small incisions into which charcoal was rubbed, probably reflect treatments for pain relief. Traces of arsenic in his hair indicate that he was exposed to the smelting of copper. His last meals included wild goat and deer meat as well as threshed and processed wheat, perhaps in the form of bread, which suggests that he lived in an agricultural community. A gash in his hand points to hand-to-hand fighting not long before his death; a flint arrow that lodged in his back and severed an artery, as well as evidence of a blow to his head, show that Otzi did not die a natural death but was killed. His attacker appears to have then pulled out the shaft of the arrow, perhaps fearing it could identify him, for no such shaft was found among his remains. So we know how Otzi died, but not why. Even so, it is about as close as we get to a particular event in history before writing.

Materials accompanying his body fill out the picture of his life. His clothing consisted of a leather loincloth and leggings, a coat of stitched animal furs, and, covering all of this, a cape of woven grass. A belt, a bearskin cap, and waterproof shoes made of bearskin and deer hide and stuffed with grass as insulation completed his outfit. An ax with a copper blade reveals that Otzi was living at the beginning of the age of metals, while stone scrapers and a flint knife indicate continued reliance on an earlier technology. He was well provisioned for a substantial journey with several small baskets, a birch bark drinking cup, several dried mushrooms, replacement materials of leather straps and sinew, a drill and a tool for sharpening flint blades, a six-foot bow and a quiver full of arrows, and a wood-framed backpack. We know that Otzi was far from his home, probably located considerably to the south of the Alpine mountain chain where he died, but no one knows why he chose to go there.

Was he a shepherd herding his flock, part of an armed party involved in a skirmish with enemies, or a solitary traveler attacked by local people?

Questions to consider as you examine the source:

■ What elements of the above description are visible in the reconstructed drawing?

■ Do you think that the inferences about Otzi's life made by scholars are justified based on the evidence available?

Source 1.4A
Otzi the Ice Man: Artist's Reconstruction

W. Smetek/STERN/Picture Press

This image shows an artist's reconstruction of the Ice Man and some of his accompanying materials.

Source 1.4B
Otzi the Ice Man's Preserved Body

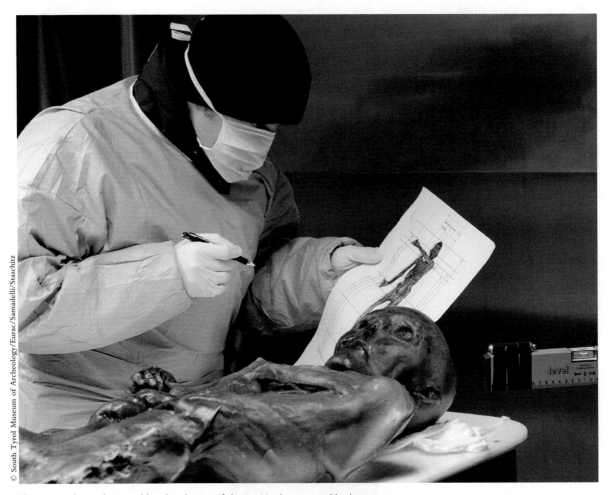

This image shows the actual head and torso of the Ice Man's preserved body.

Source 1.5
Stonehenge

Structures or buildings also offer insights into the life of people without writing. In the Neolithic age of agriculture, more large-scale stone structures, known as megaliths, appeared in various places, and settled farming communities required more elaborate dwellings, including some substantial stone fortifications. Among the most famous sites of the early agrarian era is Stonehenge, a series of earthworks accompanied by circles of standing stones located in southern England, where the Agricultural Revolution emerged around 4000 B.C.E. Construction of the Stonehenge site began around 3100 B.C.E. and continued intermittently for another 1,500 years.

Almost everything about Stonehenge has been a matter of controversy and speculation. Prominent among these debates have been the questions of motivation and function. Why was it constructed? What purposes did it serve for those early farming peoples who used it? The discovery of the cremated remains of some 240 individuals, dating to the first five centuries of its existence, has convinced some scholars that it was a burial site, perhaps for members of a single high-ranking family. It was the "domain of the dead" or an abode of the ancestors, argued one archeologist, linked ritually perhaps to the nearby village of Durrington Walls, a "land of the living" consisting of 300 to 1,000 homes.[4] Others have cast Stonehenge as an astronomical observatory, aligned with the solstices and able to predict eclipses and the movement of heavenly bodies, or perhaps a center of sun worship. Most recently, it has been depicted as "a place of pilgrimage for the sick and injured of the Neolithic world," based on the number of burials in the area that show signs of serious illness, trauma, or deformity as well as the presence of many bluestone rock chips thought to have magical healing properties.[5]

Whatever its purposes, still other controversies surround the manner of its construction. How were those huge slabs of rock, some as heavy as fifty tons and others coming from a location 240 miles away, transported to Stonehenge and put into place? Were they dragged overland or transported partway by boat along the River Avon? Or did the movement of earlier glaciers deposit them in the region?

Questions to consider as you examine the source:

- Have a look at the aerial photograph of Stonehenge. How would you describe its major features to someone who had never seen it? What questions about the site come to mind?

- What kinds of additional evidence would be most useful to scholars seeking to puzzle out the mysteries of Stonehenge?

Stonehenge

ESSAY QUESTIONS

History before Writing: How Do We Know?

1. **Comparing sources:** Which of these sources seems most useful in understanding human history before writing? Do you find that Nisa's contemporary account offers more or fewer insights than the physical remains from long ago? What are the advantages and drawbacks of each?

2. **Connecting past and present:** In what ways do these sources retain their ability to speak to people living in industrial societies of the twenty-first century? Or do they have meaning only for those who created them? Which sources do you relate to most strongly?

3. **Reflecting on speculation:** Our understanding of all of these works is highly uncertain, inviting a considerable amount of speculation, guesswork, or imagination. Why are historians willing to articulate uncertain interpretations of these ancient sources? Is this an appropriate undertaking for historians, or should scholars remain silent when the evidence does not allow them to speak with certainty and authority?

Notes

1. Gregory Curtin, *The Cave Painters* (New York: Random House, 2006), 96.

2. Ian Hodder, "Discussions with the Goddess Community," Çatalhöyük: Excavations of a Neolithic Anatolian Höyük, accessed May 14, 2015, http://www.catalhoyuk.com/library/goddess.html.

3. Quoted in Jack Linthicum, "A Journey to 9,000 Years Ago," tech-archive.net, January 17, 2008, http://sci.tech-archive.net/Archive/sci.archaeology/2008-01/msg00519.html.

4. Robin Melrose, *The Druids and King Arthur* (Jefferson, NC: McFarland, 2011), 94.

5. Adrian Croft and Golnar Motevalli, "Stonehenge May Have Been Pilgrimage Site for the Sick," Reuters, September 23, 2008, http://uk.reuters.com/article/2008/09/23/us-britain-stonehenge -idUKTRE48M0R320080923.

CHAPTER 2

THINKING THROUGH SOURCES

Social Life in the First Civilizations

The advent of writing was not only a central feature of most First Civilizations but also a great boon to later historians. Access to ancient peoples' early written records allows us some insight, in their own words, as to how these peoples lived and how they thought about their lives. Such documents, of course, tell only a small part of the story, for they most often reflect the thinking of the literate few — usually male, upper class, powerful, and well-to-do — rather than the outlook of the vast majority who lacked such privileged positions. But on occasion, we catch a glimpse of more ordinary life in these ancient texts. Furthermore, the artistic products of these civilizations sometimes allow us to witness, or perhaps to imagine, something of the life of our ancient ancestors. What follows are texts and images from the First Civilizations of Mesopotamia, Egypt, and China, all of them reflecting in some fashion the social lives of people in these First Civilizations.

Source 2.1
Law and Life in Ancient Mesopotamia

The famous Code of Hammurabi offers a window into the social life of ancient Mesopotamia. Hammurabi (r. ca. 1795–1750 B.C.E.) was the ruler of the Babylonian Empire, which for a time gave a measure of political unity to the rival cities and kingdoms of Mesopotamia. Sometime during his reign, he ordered inscribed on a large stone stele a number of laws, judgments, or decrees. They were intended, in Hammurabi's words, "to bring about the rule of righteousness in the land, to destroy the wicked and the evil-doers; so that the strong should not harm the weak . . . , to further the well-being of mankind." But since law is generally intended to cope with social problems, we can infer something about ordinary life in this ancient civilization.

Questions to consider as you examine the source:

- What distinct social groups are mentioned in the code? And what kind of social hierarchy can you discern?

- What rights did women enjoy, and to what restrictions were they subject?

- What can you infer from the code about the kind of social problems that afflicted ancient Mesopotamia?

- How would you define the principles of justice that underlay Hammurabi's code? In what different ways might twenty-first-century observers and those living at the time of Hammurabi assess that system of justice?

The Law Code of Hammurabi
ca. 1750 B.C.E.

All important

On Crime, Punishment, and Justice

2. If anyone bring an accusation against a man, and the accused go to the river and leap into the river, if he sink in the river his accuser shall take possession of his house. But if the river prove that the accused is not guilty, and he escape unhurt, then he who had brought the accusation shall be put to death, while he who leaped into the river shall take possession of the house that had belonged to his accuser. . . .

3. If anyone bring an accusation of any crime before the elders, and does not prove what he has charged, he shall, if it be a capital offense charged, be put to death. . . .

5. If a judge try a case, reach a decision, and present his judgment in writing; if later error shall appear in his decision, and it be through his own fault, then he shall pay twelve times the fine set by him in the case, and he shall be publicly removed from the judge's bench, and never again shall he sit there to render judgment. . . .

22. If anyone is committing a robbery and is caught, then he shall be put to death. . . .

196. If a man put out the eye of another man, his eye shall be put out.

197. If he break another man's bone, his bone shall be broken. . . .

On the Economy

26. If a chieftain or a man [common soldier], who has been ordered to go upon the king's highway for war does not go, but hires a mercenary, if he withholds the compensation, then shall this officer or man be put to death, and he who represented him shall take possession of his house. . . .

30. If a chieftain or a man leave his house, garden, and field and hires it out, and someone else takes possession of his house, garden, and field and uses it for three years: if the first owner return and claims his house, garden, and field, it shall not be given to him, but he who has taken possession of it and used it shall continue to use it. . . .

53. If anyone be too lazy to keep his dam in proper condition, and does not so keep it; if then the dam break and all the fields be flooded, then shall he in whose dam the break occurred be sold for money, and the money shall replace the corn [grain] which he has caused to be ruined. . . .

104. If a merchant give an agent corn, wool, oil, or any other goods to transport, the agent shall give a receipt for the amount, and compensate the merchant therefore. Then he shall obtain a receipt from the merchant for the money that he gives the merchant. . . .

122. If anyone give another silver, gold, or anything else to keep, he shall show everything to some witness, draw up a contract, and then hand it over for safe keeping. . . .

229. If a builder build a house for someone, and does not construct it properly, and the house which he built fall in and kill its owner, then that builder shall be put to death. . . .

253. If anyone agree with another to tend his field, give him seed, entrust a yoke of oxen to him, and bind him to cultivate the field, if he steal the corn or plants, and take them for himself, his hands shall be hewn off. . . .

271. If anyone hire oxen, cart, and driver, he shall pay one hundred and eighty ka of corn per day. . . .

On Class and Slavery

8. If anyone steal cattle or sheep, or an ass, or a pig or a goat, if it belong to a god or to the court, the thief shall pay thirtyfold therefore; if they belonged to a freed man of the king he shall pay tenfold; if the thief has nothing with which to pay, he shall be put to death. . . .

15. If anyone take a male or female slave of the court, or a male or female slave of a freed man, outside the city gates, he shall be put to death. . . .

17. If anyone find runaway male or female slaves in the open country and bring them to their masters, the master of the slaves shall pay him two shekels of silver. . . .

117. If anyone fail to meet a claim for debt, and sell himself, his wife, his son, and daughter for money or give them away to forced labor: they shall work for three years in the house of the man who bought them, or the proprietor, and in the fourth year they shall be set free. . . .

198. If he put out the eye of a freed man, or break the bone of a freed man, he shall pay one gold mina.

199. If he put out the eye of a man's slave, or break the bone of a man's slave, he shall pay one-half of its value. . . .

202. If anyone strike the body of a man higher in rank than he, he shall receive sixty blows with an ox-whip in public. . . .

215. If a physician make a large incision with an operating knife and cure it, or if he open a tumor [over the eye] with an operating knife, and saves the eye, he shall receive ten shekels in money.

216. If the patient be a freed man, he receives five shekels.

217. If he be the slave of someone, his owner shall give the physician two shekels. . . .

On Men and Women

110. If a "sister of a god" [an elite woman formally dedicated to the temple of a god] open a tavern, or enter a tavern to drink, then shall this woman be burned to death. . . .

128. If a man take a woman to wife, but have no intercourse with her, this woman is no wife to him.

129. If a man's wife be surprised with another man, both shall be tied and thrown into the water, but the husband may pardon his wife and the king his slaves.

130. If a man violate the wife [betrothed wife or child-wife] of another man, who has never known a man, and still lives in her father's house, and sleep with her and be surprised, this man shall be put to death, but the wife is blameless.

132. If the "finger is pointed" at a man's wife about another man, but she is not caught sleeping with the other man, she shall jump into the river for her husband. . . .

136. If anyone leave his house, run away, and then his wife go to another house, if then he return, and wishes to take his wife back: because he fled from his home and ran away, the wife of this runaway shall not return to her husband.

137. If a man wish to separate from a woman who has borne him children, or from his wife who has borne him children: then he shall give that wife her dowry, and a part of the usufruct [the

right to use] of field, garden, and property, so that she can rear her children. When she has brought up her children . . . she may then marry the man of her heart. . . .

142. If a woman quarrel with her husband, and say: "You are not congenial to me," the reasons for her prejudice must be presented. If she is guiltless, and there is no fault on her part, but he leaves and neglects her, then no guilt attaches to this woman, she shall take her dowry and go back to her father's house.

143. If she is not innocent, but leaves her husband, and ruins her house, neglecting her husband, this woman shall be cast into the water. . . .

148. If a man take a wife, and she be seized by disease, if he then desire to take a second wife, he shall not put away his wife who has been attacked by disease, but he shall keep her in the house which he has built and support her so long as she lives.

Source: *The Code of Hammurabi*, translated by L. W. King (New York, 1915).

Source 2.2
The Standard of Ur

One of the most compelling visual illustrations of ancient Mesopotamian society comes from an artifact known as the Standard of Ur. Found in a large cemetery in the Sumerian city of Ur in what is now southern Iraq, the Standard is in fact a wooden box with elaborate inlaid mosaics on two sides, each of which has three panels, or registers. It dates to about 2500 B.C.E. No one knows why it was created or what use was made of it, but for historians it has become a vivid image of Mesopotamian social life.

Each side of the Standard tells its own story. One side, often called the "peace side," depicts a prosperous, well-ordered, and very hierarchical society, in which the class differences of civilizations are sharply drawn. The upper class feasts, while the commoners offer the products of their labor. Such was the way of civilization. The other side, or "war side," of the Standard illustrates yet another aspect of Mesopotamian society, for the many wars of Mesopotamian cities and empires generated prisoners who often became slaves.

Questions to consider as you examine the source:

- What distinct occupational roles can you identify in these images?

- What major social distinctions might be inferred from the Standard of Ur?

- What other information might historians derive from this artifact?

Source 2.2A
The Standard of Ur, Peace Panel

The bottom two registers show commoners parading their agricultural produce and their animals, perhaps bringing tribute to the ruler and his entourage. The king is shown seated at the far left of the top register, in company with several servants and six seated members of the elite, each holding a raised cup. On the far right, a man is playing the lyre, perhaps accompanying a singer at the end.

Source 2.2B
The Standard of Ur, War Panel

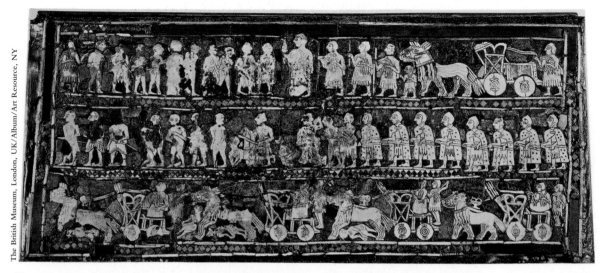

The British Museum, London, UK/Album/Art Resource, NY

The top register shows the king, large enough that his head penetrates the decorative border, standing in front of his leading warriors and his chariot. To his right stand the defeated prisoners, naked, bound, and bloody from their wounds. The middle register shows a battle scene and more prisoners, while the bottom panel presents war chariots trampling the defeated enemy.

Source 2.3
The Occupations of Old Egypt

Compared to small Paleolithic communities and later agricultural village societies, civilizations developed a far more complex division of labor and a much greater sense of social hierarchy. Such features of the First Civilizations are on display in the Egyptian text commonly known as "Be a Scribe." Dating from the Middle Kingdom period (2066–1650 B.C.E.), it was a school text that students training for administrative positions would copy in an effort to improve their writing. It also conveyed to them the exalted position of a scribe in contrast to many other occupations. One such text suggested that writing granted a kind of immortality to the scribe: "Man decays; his corpse is dust; all his kin have perished. But a book makes him remembered through the mouth of its reciter."[1]

Questions to consider as you examine the source:

- What might historians learn from this text about the occupational and social structure of Middle Kingdom Egypt?

- What does learning to write offer to a young Egyptian? What advantages of a scribal position are suggested in the document?

- What timeless frustrations of a teacher are evident in this text?

Be a Scribe
ca. 2066–1650 B.C.E.

Apply yourself to [this] noble profession.... You will find it useful.... You will be advanced by your superiors. You will be sent on a mission.... Love writing, shun dancing; then you become a worthy official.... By day write with your fingers; recite by night. Befriend the scroll, the palette. It pleases more than wine. Writing for him who knows it is better than all other professions. It pleases more than bread and beer, more than clothing and ointment. It is worth more than an inheritance in Egypt, than a tomb in the west.

Young fellow, how conceited you are! ... But though I beat you with every kind of stick, you do not listen.... You are a person fit for writing, though you have not yet known a woman. Your heart discerns, your fingers are skilled, your mouth is apt for reciting....

But though I spend the day telling you "Write," it seems like a plague to you....

See for yourself with your own eye. The occupations lie before you.

The washerman's day is going up, going down. All his limbs are weak, [from] whitening his neighbor's clothes every day, from washing their linen.

The maker of pots is smeared with soil.... [H]e is like one who lives in the bog.

The cobbler mingles with vats. His odor is penetrating. His hands are red . . . , like one who is smeared with blood. . . .

The watchman prepares garlands and polishes vase-stands. He spends a night of toil just as one on whom the sun shines.

The merchants travel downstream and upstream. They are as busy as can be, carrying goods from one town to another. They supply him who has wants. But the tax collectors carry off the gold, that most precious of metals.

The ships' crews from every house [of commerce], they receive their loads. They depart from Egypt for Syria, and each man's god is with him. [But] not one of them says: "We shall see Egypt again!"

[The] outworker who is in the fields, his is the toughest of all the jobs. He spends the day loaded with his tools, tied to his toolbox. When he returns home at night, he is loaded with the tool-box and the timbers, his drinking mug, and his whetstones. . . .

Let me also expound to you the situation of the peasant, that other tough occupation. [Comes] the inundation and soaks him . . . , he attends to his equipment. By day he cuts his farming tools; by night he twists rope. Even his midday hour he spends on farm labor. He equips himself to go to the field as if he were a warrior.... When he reaches his field he finds [it?] broken up. He spends time cultivating, and the snake is after him. It finishes off the seed as it is cast to the ground. He does not see a green blade. He does three plowings with borrowed grain. His wife has gone down to the merchants and found nothing for barter. . . .

If you have any sense, be a scribe. If you have learned about the peasant, you will not be able to be one.... Look, I instruct you to ... make you become one whom the king trusts; to make you gain entrance to treasury and granary. To make you receive the shipload at the gate of the granary. To make you issue the offerings on feast days. You are dressed in fine clothes; you own horses. Your boat is on the river; you are supplied with attendants. You stride about inspecting. A mansion is built in your town. You have a powerful office, given you by the king. Male and female slaves are about you. Those who are in the fields grasp your hand, on plots that you have made. . . . Put the writings in your heart, and you will be protected from all kinds of toil. You will become a worthy official.

Do you not recall the [fate of] the unskilled man? His name is not known. He is ever burdened [like an ass carrying things] in front of the scribe who knows what he is about.

Come, [let me tell] you the woes of the soldier, and how many are his superiors: the general, the troop-commander, the officer who leads, the standard-bearer, the lieutenant, the scribe, the commander of fifty, and the garrison-captain. They go in and out in the halls of the palace, saying: "Get laborers!" He is awakened at any hour. One is after him as [after] a donkey. He toils until the Aten sets in his darkness of night. He is hungry, his belly hurts; he is dead while yet alive. When he receives the grain-ration, having been released from duty, it is not good for grinding.

He is called up for Syria. He may not rest. There are no clothes, no sandals. . . . His march is uphill through mountains. He drinks water every third day; it is smelly and tastes of salt. His body is ravaged by illness. The enemy comes, surrounds him with missiles, and life recedes from him. He is told: "Quick, forward, valiant soldier! Win for yourself a good name!" He does not know what he is about. His body is weak, his legs fail him. When victory is won, the captives are handed over to his majesty, to be taken to Egypt. . . . His wife and children are in their village; he dies and does not reach it. If he comes out alive, he is worn out from marching. . . .

Be a scribe, and be spared from soldiering! You call and one says: "Here I am." You are safe from torments. Every man seeks to raise himself up. Take note of it!

Source: *Ancient Egyptian Literature: Volume 1: The Old and Middle Kingdoms* by Miriam Lichtheim, © 2006 by the Regents of the University of California. Published by the University of California Press. Used by permission of the University of California Press.

Source 2.4
The Social Relationships of Egyptian Agriculture

This Egyptian image from the fourteenth century B.C.E. comes from the tomb of a scribe named Menna. Much like the scribes described in Source 2.3, Menna held an important official role, though he was a commoner by birth. Known as the "scribe of the fields," he supervised agricultural lands owned by various temples, which produced grain for the royal granaries. So Menna measured the fields, recorded the yields, and generally oversaw the work.

This scene records various phases of agricultural work. The bottom panel shows men carrying baskets of grain, while two young girls and a small boy, perhaps slaves, fight over the droppings. Three old men, indicated by their gray hair, relax under a tree, one of them playing an instrument and another leaning on a stick. In the middle panel, oxen trample the grain to separate the seed from the straw, while several men winnow it, separating the grain from the chaff. At the far left, Menna supervises the operation. In the top panel, Menna, surrounded by hieroglyphs (Egypt's written script), oversees the beating of one worker while another seems to plead for him. And at the far right, a loaded boat carries away the grain.

Questions to consider as you examine the source:

■ What occupational or social groups can you identify in this image? What distinguishes individuals who are working from the others?

■ What might the author of "Be a Scribe" have to say about these occupations?

■ Many of the images of Menna in his tomb were disfigured, while those of his wife remained intact. Can you infer why he might have incurred such hostility?

Agricultural Scenes from the Tomb of Menna

Luxor, Thebes, Egypt/Borromeo/Art Resource, NY

Source 2.5

Social Life in Ancient China

The best window on social life in the early civilization of China comes from a text known as *The Book of Songs*. Originating as oral traditions during the Shang and Zhou dynasties (1600–771 B.C.E.), these odes or poems were sometimes collected by rulers seeking to know something of the life of their people. Tradition has it that Confucius himself compiled them into their present form of 305 individual poems. More likely, educated scholars at the Zhou dynasty court reworked folk songs and traditions into a more elegant literary expression. By the time of the Han dynasty (206 B.C.E.–220 C.E.), they had become a part of the *Five Classics* of Confucian orthodoxy, studied by generations of Chinese scholars well into the twentieth century. Many of the poems in *The Book of Songs* expressed the voices of ordinary Chinese people — peasants, soldiers, officials, and wives. Quite a few of them reflected the perspective of women.

Questions to consider as you examine the source:

■ What difficulties of life in early China do these selections disclose? Which of them reflect the specific conditions of ancient Chinese civilization, and which give voice to more broadly human longings?

■ What distinct social groups and conflicts are disclosed in these passages?

■ How are the more personal relationships of family, clan, marriage, and love articulated in these passages? To what extent do you think they offset the difficulties and disappointments of ordinary life?

The Book of Songs
ca. 1046–771 B.C.E.

Selection A: The Perspective of Soldiers

[*The hardship of soldiers serving on the frontier. It was common for only sons to be excused from military service in order to care for their aged parents, but this poem suggests that this provision was not always honored.*]

To the Minister of War:

Why be we, the teeth and talons of the King,
Moved about, in miserable case,
With no longer an abiding place?

Why be we, the braves, the talons of the King,
Moved about, in miserable plight,
With the end still hidden from our sight?

Surely here is lack of judgment shown.
Why transport us to this misery,
Who have mothers managing the meals alone?

Selection B: The Perspective of a Local Official

[*The burden of a local official and his submission to the will of Heaven.*]

Out by the northern gate I go my way,
Bearing a load of sorrow and of care;
Vulgarly poor am I, and sore bestead,
And of my hardships all are unaware.

On me devolves the business of the king,
On me official burdens fast encroach;
On me, at home, arriving from abroad,
My household all conspire to heap reproach

All urgent is the business of the king;
Official cares press on me more and more.
And when at home, arriving from abroad,
My household one and all thrust at me sore.

Ah, so indeed,
Yet Heaven hath so decreed
What therefore can I say?

Selection C: The Perspective of Peasants

[*A peasant's comparison of exploiting landlords and tax collectors to huge rats and a dream of a brighter future.*]

Monster rats! O monster rats!
Eat not our millet, we implore.
Three years we've borne with you,
And still our presence you ignore.
Now we abandon you,
And to yon pleasant lands repair.
O pleasant lands! O pleasant lands!
A refuge have we surely there.

O monster rats! O monster rats!
Devour not all our crops of wheat.
Three years we've borne with you,
Still with no mercy do we meet.
Now we abandon you,

And take to yon glad Land our flight.
Gladsome Land! O gladsome Land!
There justice shall we have, and right.

Monster rats! O monster rats!
Devour not all our springing grain.
Three years we've borne with you,
Nor heed you still our toil and pain.
Now we abandon you
For brighter plains that yonder lie.
O brighter plains! O brighter plains!
Whose, then, will be the constant cry?

Selection D: The Perspective of Family or Clan

[*A celebration of the delights of family and clan, while comparing them to relationships with friends.*]

Is not the cherry-tree, all around,
With opening blossoms grandly crowned?
So, nowhere in the world of men
Is the like of clansmen found.

Bereaved by death in ways we dread,
How is the clansman's heart oppressed!
O'er hill and dale, amid heaps of dead,
Brother for brother makes his quest.

Though brothers may have private feud,
They fight (as one) the alien foe;
And each has friends, both sure and good,
But friends to help? Ah, surely no!

Make thee a feast, make all complete,
And drink thy heart's content of wine;
'Tis when the band of clansmen meet
That mirth and childlike joy combine.

Union with wife and child is sweet,
Sweet as when lutes in concert blend;
'Tis when united clansmen meet
That mirth and concord know no end.

Selection E: The Perspective of a Wife Betrayed

[*The lament of a woman cast off when her husband found another wife.*]

When East winds blow unceasingly,
They bring but gloominess and rain.
Strive, strive to live unitedly,
And every angry thought restrain.
So, while unsullied was my name,
I should have lived with you till death.

With slow, slow step I took the road,
My inmost heart rebelling sore.
You came not far with me indeed,
You only saw me to the door.
Ay, feast there with your new-found bride,
Well-pleased, as when fond brothers meet.

And you can show me no kind care,
Nay, treated like a foe am I!
My virtue stood but in your way,
Like traders' goods that none will buy.

Once it was feared we could not live;
In your reverses, then I shared;
And now, when fortune smiles on you,
To very poison I'm compared.

Rude fits of anger you have shown,
Now left me to be sorely tried.
Ah, you forget those days gone by,
When you came nestling to my side!

Source: William Jennings, *The Shi King: The Old "Poetry Classic" of the Chinese* (London: George Routledge and Sons, 1891), A:203, B:67–68, C:126, D:176–77, E:62–64, https://archive.org/stream /shikingoldpoetry00jennuoft#page/n3/mode/2up.

Source 2.6
Socializing with Ancestors

Social life in ancient China, and in many other places as well, was not limited to the living. Rulers and peasants alike understood themselves to be as closely related to their departed ancestors as to their contemporaries. One later Chinese ruler constructed a huge underground city in which he would continue to rule after death, in association with soldiers, officials, and entertainers, amid the many objects with which he was familiar in life (see Chapter 3). People in far more modest circumstances frequently offered food and drink, sometimes whole banquets, to nourish their ancestors, hoping for their support and assistance in the vagaries of life.

This exquisite bronze bowl, a ritual vessel for making such offerings to ancestors and dating to about 1050 B.C.E., was commissioned by Mei Situ Yi, an apparently prosperous military official who had been involved in the overthrow of the Shang dynasty by the forces of the new Zhou dynasty. An inscription in the bottom of the bowl tells us that it was "in honor of his late father," also a warrior. Such vessels usually came in sets, with each one having a very particular role in the banquets that allowed the living to keep in touch with the dead. Among the elite, however, they were also sometimes buried with the deceased to allow him to organize such banquets in the afterlife for his own ancestors.[2]

Questions to consider as you examine the source:

- The casting of such bowls was a very time-consuming and expensive process. What does this suggest about the status of those who could afford such an item?

- What physical features of the bowl do you find most striking? Notice especially the handles, each of which depicts a large beast swallowing a bird. Might you care to speculate about the meaning of such an image?

- How might such items be useful to historians seeking to reconstruct the history of ancient China?

Socializing with Ancestors: Bronze Gui

Social Life in the First Civilizations

1. **Making comparisons:** If you came across these sources in one place, would you be more struck by the similarities or the differences of the civilizations they represent?

2. **Considering past and present:** What elements of social life from these earliest of civilizations still resonate in the twenty-first century? What elements remain strange or unfamiliar to modern sensibilities?

3. **Reading between the lines:** Historians often use documents to obtain insights or information that the authors did not intend to convey. How might Sources 2.1, 2.3, and 2.5 be used in this fashion? What are the advantages and dangers in this use of ancient texts?

4. **Considering written and visual sources:** What kind of insights can we derive from visual sources that are not available in written documents?

Notes

1. Miriam Lichtheim, *Ancient Egyptian Literature* (Berkeley: University of California Press, 1975), 2:177.

2. "Chinese Zhou Ritual Vessel," *A History of the World in 100 Objects*, No. 23, BBC, http://www.bbc.co.uk /ahistoryoftheworld/objects/9ncaOZABRHO5tcKeacBlJQ.

CHAPTER 3

THINKING THROUGH SOURCES

Political Authority in Second-Wave Civilizations

States, empires, and their rulers are surely not the whole story of the human past, although historians have sometimes treated them as though they were. But they are important because their actions shaped the lives of many millions of people. The city-states of ancient Greece, the Roman Empire, the emerging Chinese empire of the Qin dynasty, and the Indian empire of the Mauryan dynasty — these were among the impressive political structures of the second-wave era in Eurasia. Rulers in each of these regions sought to establish or maintain their authority by mobilizing and promoting a variety of ideas that gave legitimacy to their regimes. The sources in this collection explore how rulers sought to advertise and strengthen their legitimacy and authority. Keep in mind that each of the sources represents an idealized image of political authority rather than an "objective" discussion of how these political systems actually operated. They reflect how rulers, with the help of their advisers, expressed their values and their self-image even as they created mythologies and rituals that endured far longer than those who generated these texts and works of art and propaganda.

Source 3.1
Behistun Inscription
ca. 500 B.C.E.

From the Persian Empire comes an impressive representation of political power: a monumental sculptural program and lengthy multilingual inscription located on a limestone cliff some 300 feet above the ground in western Iran. Known as the Behistun Inscription, this monument was commissioned by the emperor Darius the Great (r. 522–486 B.C.E.) to celebrate his many victories over foreign enemies and domestic rebels alike. The central figure in the carving is Darius himself, the third from the left, holding a bow as a symbol of rulership with his foot on the chest of one of the rebels whom he had crushed. To the right stands a line of nine captives roped at the neck with their hands tied behind them, who represent other rebels or conquered peoples. To the left of Darius are two of his leading generals, who have the honor of ritually carrying the monarch's bow and lance respectively. Hovering over the entire scene is the Faravahar, the ancient Near Eastern winged disk symbol, which had come to represent Ahura Mazda and the Zoroastrian tradition.

Accompanying this image are five columns of inscriptions recounting in three languages Darius's triumphs during the first three years of his reign and asserting that they were accomplished "by the grace of Ahura Mazda," the great benevolent Deity of Zoroastrianism (see photo of Zoroastrian Fire Altar on page 166 of the main text). Reproduced here are the opening lines of the inscription where Darius offers an autobiography of himself and part of the conclusion where he summarizes his accomplishments and asserts the righteousness of his actions. The intervening passages recount individual victories over his enemies, as do several passages added to the end.

Questions to consider as you examine the source:

- What message did Darius seek to convey in commissioning this work?

- How does this monument present the sources of political authority in the Persian Empire?

- What does the written text add to your understanding of the visual components of this monument?

Source 3.1A
Behistun Inscription

De Agostini Picture Library/W. Buss/Bridgeman Images

Source 3.1B
Behistun Inscription
ca. 500 B.C.E.

I am Darius, the great king, king of kings, the king of Persia, the king of countries, the son of Hystaspes, the grandson of Arsames, the Achaemenid.

King Darius says: Eight of my dynasty were kings before me; I am the ninth. Nine in succession we have been kings.

King Darius says: By the grace of Ahura Mazda am I king; Ahura Mazda has granted me the kingdom.

King Darius says: These are the countries which are subject unto me, and by the grace of Ahura Mazda I became king of them: [There follows a list of states that he conquered.]

King Darius says: These are the countries which are subject to me; by the grace of Ahura Mazda they became subject to me; they brought tribute unto me. Whatsoever commands have been laid on them by me, by night or by day, have been performed by them.

King Darius says: Within these lands, whosoever was a friend, him have I surely protected; whosoever was hostile, him have I utterly destroyed.

King Darius says: Ahura Mazda has granted unto me this empire. Ahura Mazda brought me help, until I gained this empire; by the grace of Ahura Mazda do I hold this empire.

[The intervening passages record Darius's triumphs over foreign enemies and domestic rebellions.]

King Darius says: This is what I have done. By the grace of Ahura Mazda have I always acted. After I became king, I fought nineteen battles in a single year and by the grace of Ahura Mazda I overthrew nine kings and I made them captive.

King Darius says: As to these provinces which revolted, lies made them revolt, so that they deceived the people. Then Ahura Mazda delivered them into my hand; and I did unto them according to my will.

King Darius says: You who shall be king hereafter, protect yourself vigorously from lies; punish the liars well, if thus you shall think, "May my country be secure!"

King Darius says: This is what I have done, by the grace of Ahura Mazda have I always acted. Whosoever shall read this inscription hereafter, let that which I have done be believed. You must not hold it to be lies.

King Darius says: Those who were the former kings, as long as they lived, by them was not done thus as by the favor of Ahura Mazda was done by me in one and the same year.

King Darius says: Now let what has been done by me convince you. For the sake of the people, do not conceal it. If you do not conceal this edict but if you publish it to the world, then may Ahura Mazda be your friend, may your family be numerous, and may you live long.

King Darius says: If you conceal this edict and do not publish it to the world, may Ahura Mazda slay you and may your house cease.

King Darius says: This is what I have done in one single year; by the grace of Ahura Mazda have I always acted. Ahura Mazda brought me help, and the other gods, all that there are.

King Darius says: On this account Ahura Mazda brought me help, and all the other gods, all that there are, because I was not wicked, nor was I a liar, nor was I a despot, neither I nor any of my family. I have ruled according to righteousness. Neither to the weak nor to the powerful did I do wrong. Whosoever helped my house, him I favored; he who was hostile, him I destroyed.

King Darius says: You who may be king hereafter, whosoever shall be a liar or a rebel, or shall not be friendly, punish him!

Source: *The Sculptures and Inscription of Darius the Great on the Rock of Behistûn in Persia* (London: British Museum, 1907), full text available electronically at https://archive.org/details/sculptures inscri00brituoft.

Source 3.2
In Praise of Athenian Democracy

The Greeks of Athens generated political ideas that have long been celebrated in the West, although they were exceptional even in the small world of classical Greece. The best-known expression of praise for Athenian democracy comes from Pericles, the most prominent Athenian leader during the fifth century B.C.E. Sometimes called the "first citizen of Athens," Pericles initiated the grand building projects that still grace the Acropolis and led his city in its military struggles with archrival Sparta. To his critics, he was a populist, manipulating the masses to enhance his own power, and an

Athenian imperialist whose aggressive policies ultimately ruined the city. His famous speech in praise of Athens was delivered around 431–430 B.C.E. at the end of the first year of the Peloponnesian War against Sparta. The setting was a public funeral service for Athenian citizens who had died in that conflict. Pericles' oration was recorded by the Greek historian Thucydides (thoo-SIHD-ih-dees), who was probably present at that event.

Questions to consider as you examine the source:

- Does Pericles' argument for democracy derive from fundamental principles, such as human equality, or from the practical benefits that arise from such a system of government?

- What kind of citizens does Pericles believe democracy produces? Keep in mind that not everyone shared this idealized view of Athenian democracy. How might critics have responded to Pericles' arguments?

- Although Pericles praised Athenian military prowess, his city lost the Peloponnesian War. In what ways does this affect your assessment of his arguments?

PERICLES

Funeral Oration
431–430 B.C.E.

Our form of government does not enter into rivalry with the institutions of others. We do not copy our neighbors, but are an example to them. It is true that we are called a democracy, for the administration is in the hands of the many and not of the few. But while the law secures equal justice to all alike in their private disputes, the claim of excellence is also recognized; and when a citizen is in any way distinguished, he is preferred to the public service, not as a matter of privilege, but as the reward of merit. Neither is poverty a bar, but a man may benefit his country whatever be the obscurity of his condition. There is no exclusiveness in our public life, and in our private intercourse we are not suspicious of one another, nor angry with our neighbor if he does what he likes. . . . While we are thus unconstrained in our private intercourse, a spirit of reverence pervades our public acts; we are prevented from doing wrong by respect for the authorities and for the laws. . . .

And we have not forgotten to provide for our weary spirits many relaxations from toil; we have regular games and sacrifices throughout the year; our homes are beautiful and elegant; and the delight which we daily feel in all these things helps to banish melancholy. Because of the greatness of our city the fruits of the whole earth flow in upon us; so that we enjoy the goods of other countries as freely as of our own.

Then, again, our military training is in many respects superior to that of our adversaries. Our city is thrown open to the world, and we never expel a foreigner or prevent him from seeing or learning anything of which the secret if revealed to an enemy might profit him. We rely not upon management or trickery, but upon our own hearts and hands. And in the matter of education, whereas they from early youth are always undergoing laborious exercises which are to make them brave, we live at ease, and yet are equally ready to face the perils which they face. . . .

For we are lovers of the beautiful, yet simple in our tastes, and we cultivate the mind without loss of manliness. . . . To avow poverty with us is no disgrace; the true disgrace is in doing nothing to avoid it. An Athenian citizen does not neglect the state because he takes care of his own household; and even those of us who are engaged in business have a very fair idea of politics. We alone regard a man who takes no interest in public affairs, not as a harmless, but as a useless character; and if few of us are originators, we are all sound judges of a policy. The great impediment to action is, in our opinion, not discussion, but the want of that knowledge which is gained by discussion preparatory to action. For we have a peculiar power of thinking before we act and of acting too, whereas other men are courageous from ignorance but hesitate upon reflection. And they are surely to be esteemed the bravest spirits who, having the clearest sense both of the pains and pleasures of life, do not on that account shrink from danger. . . .

To sum up: I say that Athens is the school of Hellas, and that the individual Athenian in his own person seems to have the power of adapting himself to the most varied forms of action with the utmost versatility and grace. . . .

For we have compelled every land and every sea to open a path for our valor, and have everywhere planted eternal memorials of our friendship and of our enmity. Such is the city for whose sake these men nobly fought and died; they could not bear the thought that she might be taken from them; and every one of us who survive should gladly toil on her behalf.

Source: Benjamin Jowett, *Thucydides, Translated into English, to Which Is Prefixed an Essay on Inscriptions and a Note on the Geography of Thucydides*, 2nd ed. (Oxford: Clarendon Press, 1900), bk. 2, paras. 37–41.

Source 3.3
Statue of Augustus

This statue of Augustus, the first of the Roman emperors (r. 27 B.C.E.–14 C.E.), was probably created shortly after his death, though based on a somewhat earlier bronze original. It symbolized a new era of peace and abundance in Roman history, following a century of turmoil and civil war. Here Augustus is "imperator" or military commander, wearing a breastplate and with his right arm extended as if addressing his troops. The statue was clearly intended to commemorate the victory of Augustus over the Parthian Empire, centered in Persia, in 20 B.C.E., a triumph that reversed several earlier Roman defeats. The central relief on the breastplate shows the Parthian ruler (on the right) returning to a Roman military figure the battle standard that the Parthians had seized thirty-three years before. "I compelled the Parthians to return the spoils and standards of three Roman armies," Augustus declared, "and humbly to beg the friendship of the Roman people."[1]

The other figures from Roman mythology on the breastplate represent the ordered, peaceful, stable, and bountiful world that the defeat of the Parthians promised. Cupid or Eros, riding a dolphin next to Augustus's right leg in the statue, evokes his mother, Venus, often said to be an ancestor of Augustus. Notice that the military figure of Augustus is strangely barefoot, a portrayal usually associated with gods and heroes.

Questions to consider as you examine the source:

■ What does the statue suggest about the basis of Augustus's legitimacy as a ruler? What kind of future for the empire does the statue evoke?

■ Although Augustus resisted being portrayed as divine, the statue is laced with religious imagery. What does this imagery suggest about the way Augustus was coming to be viewed?

■ Which elements of the statue suggest a realistic portrayal of Augustus, and which show an idealized image of him? Notice particularly his face and posture. What sensibility is the artist seeking to convey?

Source 3.3A
Augustus Statue

Braccio Nuovo, Museo Chiaramonti, Vatican Museums/Scala/Art Resource, NY

Source 3.3B
Augustus Statue: The Breastplate

This breastplate contains various figures from Roman mythology. At the top left is the sun god Sol driving a chariot, while the top right shows the moon goddess Luna as well as Aurora, the winged goddess of dawn, pouring dew from her jug. Between them Caelus, the sky god, spreads out the heavens, and at the bottom of the breastplate the earth goddess cradles two babies and holds a cornucopia overflowing with fruit.

Source 3.4
Governing a Chinese Empire

As the Roman Empire was taking shape in the Mediterranean basin, a powerful Chinese empire emerged in East Asia. More than in the Roman world, the political ideas and practices of imperial China drew on the past. The notion of China as a unified state ruled by a single sage/emperor who mediated between Heaven and the human realm had an ancient pedigree. After a long period of political fragmentation, known as the era of warring states, such a unified Chinese state took shape once again during the short-lived Qin dynasty (221–206 B.C.E.), led by its formidable ruler Shihuangdi. That state operated under a version of Legalism, a political philosophy that found expression in the writings of Han Fei (280–233 B.C.E.) and that in large measure guided the practices of Shihuangdi and the Qin dynasty. Han Fei's Legalist thinking was discredited by the brutality and excesses of Shihuangdi's reign, and the Han dynasty that followed was sharply critical of his ideas, favoring instead the "government by morality" approach of Confucianism. Nonetheless, Han Fei's emphasis on the importance of laws and the need to enforce them influenced all succeeding Chinese dynasties.

Questions to consider as you examine the source:

■ Why is Han Fei's approach to governing China referred to as Legalism? According to him, what is required for effective government?

■ What are the "two handles"?

■ What view of human nature underpins Han Fei's argument?

The Writings of Master Han Fei
Third Century B.C.E.

No state is forever strong or forever weak. If those who would uphold the law are strong, the state will be strong; if they are weak, the state will be weak. . . .

In the present age, he who can put an end to private scheming and make men uphold the public law will see his people secure and his state well ordered; he who can block selfish pursuits and enforce the public law will see his army growing stronger and his enemies weakening. Find men who have a clear understanding of what is beneficial to the nation and a feeling for the system of laws and regulations, and place them in charge of the lesser officials; then the ruler can never be deceived by lies and falsehoods. . . .

A truly enlightened ruler uses the law to select men for him; he does not choose them himself. He uses the law to weigh their merits; he does not attempt to judge them for himself. Hence men of true worth will not be able to hide their talents, nor spoilers to gloss over their faults. Men cannot advance on the basis of praise alone, nor be driven from court by calumny [false charges]. . . .

What the law has decreed the wise man cannot dispute nor the brave man venture to contest. When faults are to be punished, the highest minister cannot escape; when good is to be rewarded, the lowest peasant must not be passed over. Hence, for correcting the faults of superiors, chastising the misdeeds of subordinates, restoring order, exposing error, checking excesses, remedying evil, and unifying the standards of the people, nothing can compare to law. . . . If penalties are heavy, men dare not use high position to abuse the humble; if laws are clearly defined, superiors will be honored and their rights will not be invaded. . . . Were the ruler of men to discard law and follow his private whim, then all distinction between high and low would cease to exist.

The enlightened ruler controls his ministers by means of two handles alone. The two handles are punishment and favor. What do I mean by punishment and favor? To inflict mutilation and death on men is called punishment; to bestow honor and reward is called favor. Those who act as ministers fear the penalties and hope to profit by the rewards. Hence if the ruler wields his punishments and favors, the ministers will fear his sternness and flock to receive his benefits. But the evil ministers of the age are different. They cajole the ruler into letting them inflict punishments themselves on men they hate and bestow rewards on men they like. Now if the ruler of men does not insist on reserving to himself the right to dispense profit in the form of rewards and show his sternness in punishments, but instead hands them out on the advice of his ministers, then the people of the state will all fear the ministers and hold the ruler in contempt, will flock to the ministers and desert the ruler. This is the danger that arises when the ruler loses control of punishments and favors.

Source: *Basic Writings of Mo Tzu, Hsün Tzu, and Han Fei Tzu* by Mo, Di et al., translated by Burton Watson. Copyright © 1963, 1964 Columbia University Press. Reprinted with permission of the publisher.

Source 3.5
Qin Shihuangdi Funerary Complex

Surely the most stunning representation of political power during the second-wave era derived from China and expressed the grand conception of empire associated with Qin Shihuangdi, the so-called First Emperor (r. 221–210 B.C.E.). In his view, the empire he created was to be universal, even cosmic, in scope. In tours throughout his vast realm, he offered sacrifices to the various spirits, bringing them, as well as the rival kingdoms of China, into a state of unity and harmony. Qin Shihuangdi saw himself in the line of ancient sage kings, who had originally given order to the world. But the empire was also to be an eternal realm. The emperor vigorously pursued personal immortality, seeking out pills, herbs, and potions believed to convey eternal life and sending expeditions to the mythical Isles of the Immortals, thought to lie off the east coast of China. All of this found expression in the vast funerary complex constructed for Qin Shihuangdi during his lifetime near the modern city of Xian.

In early 1974, some Chinese peasants digging a well stumbled across a small corner of that complex, leading to what has become perhaps the most celebrated archeological discovery of the twentieth century. In subsequent and continuing excavations, archeologists have uncovered thousands of life-size ceramic statues of soldiers of various ranks, arrayed for battle and equipped with real weapons. Other statues portrayed officials, acrobats, musicians, wrestlers, horses, bronze chariots, birds, and more — all designed to accompany Qin Shihuangdi into the afterlife.

This amazing discovery, however, was only a very small part of an immense tomb complex covering some fifty-six square kilometers and centered on the still-unexcavated burial mound of Qin Shihuangdi. Begun in 246 B.C.E. and still incomplete when Shihuangdi died in 210 B.C.E., the construction of this gigantic complex was described by the great Chinese historian Sima Qian about a century later:

> As soon as the First Emperor became king of Qin, excavations and build-ing had been started at Mount Li, while after he won the empire, more than 700,000 conscripts from all parts of the country worked there. They dug through three subterranean streams and poured molten copper for the outer coffin, and the tomb was filled with . . . palaces, pavilions, and offices as well as fine vessels, precious stones, and rarities. Artisans were or-dered to fix up crossbows so that any thief breaking in would be shot. All the country's streams, the Yellow River and the Yangtze were reproduced in quicksilver [mercury] and by some mechanical means made to flow into a miniature ocean. The heavenly constellations were above and the regions of the earth below.[2]

Buried with the First Emperor were many of the workers who had died or were killed during construction, as well as sacrificed aristocrats and concubines.

This massive project was no mere monument to a deceased ruler. In a culture that believed the living and the dead formed a single com-munity, Qin Shihuangdi's tomb complex was a parallel society, complete with walls, palaces, cemeteries, demons, spirits, soldiers, administrators, entertainers, calendars, texts, divination records, and the luxurious objects appropriate to royalty. The tomb mound itself was like a mountain, a geographic feature that in Chinese thinking was home to gods, spirits, and immortals. From this mound, Qin Shihuangdi would rule forever over his vast domain, although invisible to the living.

Questions to consider as you examine the source:

■ How does the fact that this funerary complex was largely invisible to the general public affect your understanding of its function? How might ordinary Chinese have viewed the construction of this complex even before it was completed?

■ To what extent is the conception of political authority reflected in this funerary complex in keeping with the ideas of Han Fei in Source 3.4? How might it challenge those ideas?

■ How do you understand the religious or cosmic dimension of Chinese political thinking as reflected in this tomb complex?

Source 3.5A
Qin Shihuangdi Funerary Complex

Tomb of Qin shi Huang Di, Xianyang, China/Bridgeman Images

The largest pit is now covered with a canopy and conveys something of the massive size of this undertaking. Located about a mile east of Qin Shihuangdi's burial mound, this ceramic army, replete with horses and chariots, faced the pass in the mountains from which enemies might be expected. Some six thousand terra-cotta figures have been uncovered and painstakingly pieced together in this pit alone.

Source 3.5B

Archer

akg-images

Scholars have long been impressed with the apparent individuality of these terra-cotta figures, and some have argued that they were actually modeled on particular living soldiers. More recent research suggests, however, that they were "an early feat of mass production."[3] Well-organized workshops produced a limited variety of face shapes, body parts, hairstyles, and uniforms, which were then assembled in various combinations and slightly reworked to convey an impression of individuality. This archer is typical of the careful workmanship that gave the illusion that these statues were modeled on actual soldiers.

Source 3.5C
Bronze Horse-Drawn Cart

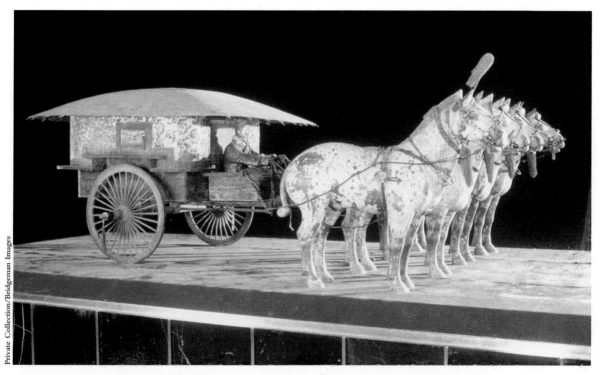

This exquisitely detailed bronze carriage, pulled by four horses, was not part of the terra-cotta army. Rather, it was found some distance away, quite close to the actual burial place of the emperor. The compartment is decorated inside and out with geometric and cloud patterns, while the round roof, perhaps, represents the sun, the sky, or the heavens above. Perhaps this carriage was intended to allow the emperor to tour his realm in the afterlife, much as he had done while alive. Or perhaps it served a one-time purpose to transport the emperor's soul into the afterlife.

Source 3.6
Governing an Indian Empire

Among the rulers of the classical era, Ashoka, of India's Mauryan dynasty (r. 268–232 B.C.E.), surely stands out, both for the personal transformation he experienced and for the benevolent philosophy of government that he subsequently articulated. Ashoka's career as emperor began in a familiar fashion — ruthless consolidation of his own power and vigorous expansion of the state's frontiers. A particularly bloody battle against the state of Kalinga marked a turning point in his reign. Apparently repulsed by the destruction,

Ashoka converted to Buddhism and turned his attention to more peaceful and tolerant ways of governing his huge empire. His edicts and advice, inscribed throughout his realm on rocks and pillars, outlined this distinctive approach to imperial governance.

The following source provides samples of instructions from Ashoka, who is referred to as King Piyadasi, or the Beloved of the Gods. The term *dhamma*, used frequently in edicts of Ashoka, refers to the "way" or the "truth" that is embodied in religious teachings.

Although Ashoka's reputation as an enlightened ruler has persisted to this day, his policies ultimately were not very successful. Shortly after Ashoka's death, the Mauryan Empire broke apart into a more common Indian pattern of competing regional states that rose and fell with some regularity. Of course, Qin Shihuangdi's much harsher Legalist policies were also unsuccessful, at least in maintaining his dynasty, which lasted a mere fifteen years.

Questions to consider as you examine the source:

■ How would you describe Ashoka's philosophy of state?

■ What specific changes did Ashoka make in state policies and practices?

■ How might Han Fei have responded to Ashoka's ideas?

ASHOKA

The Rock Edicts

ca. 268–232 B.C.E.

Beloved-of-the-Gods, King Piyadasi, conquered the Kalingas eight years after his coronation. One hundred and fifty thousand were deported, one hundred thousand were killed, and many more died [from other causes]. After the Kalingas had been conquered, Beloved-of-the-Gods came to feel a strong inclination towards the Dhamma, a love for the Dhamma and for instruction in Dhamma. Now Beloved-of-the-Gods feels deep remorse for having conquered the Kalingas. . . .

Now Beloved-of-the-Gods thinks that even those who do wrong should be forgiven where forgiveness is possible.

Even the forest people, who live in Beloved-of-the-Gods' domain, are entreated and reasoned with to act properly. They are told that despite his remorse Beloved-of-the-Gods has the power to punish them if necessary, so that they should be ashamed of their wrong and not be killed. Truly, Beloved-of-the-Gods desires non-injury, restraint, and impartiality to all beings, even where wrong has been done.

Now it is conquest by Dhamma that Beloved-of-the-Gods considers to be the best conquest. . . .

I have had this Dhamma edict written so that my sons and great-grandsons may not consider making new conquests, or that if military conquests are made, that they be done with forbearance and light punishment, or better still, that they consider making conquest by Dhamma only, for that bears fruit in this world and the next. May all their intense devotion be given to this which has a result in this world and the next.

1. Here (in my domain) no living beings are to be slaughtered or offered in sacrifice. . . .

Formerly, in the kitchen of Beloved-of-the-Gods, King Piyadasi, hundreds of thousands of animals were killed every day to make curry. But now with the writing of this Dhamma edict only three creatures, two peacocks and a deer are killed, and the deer not always. And in time, not even these three creatures will be killed.

2. . . . [E]verywhere has Beloved-of-the-Gods . . . made provision for two types of medical treatment: medical treatment for humans and medical treatment for animals. Wherever medical herbs suitable for humans or animals are not available, I have had them imported and grown. . . . Along roads I have had wells dug and trees planted for the benefit of humans and animals.

3. Everywhere in my domain the [royal officers] shall go on inspection tours every five years for the purpose of Dhamma instruction and also to conduct other business. Respect for mother and father is good, generosity to friends, acquaintances, relatives, Brahmans and ascetics is good, not killing living beings is good, moderation in spending and moderation in saving is good.

4. In the past, for many hundreds of years, killing or harming living beings and improper behavior toward relatives, and improper behavior toward Brahmans and ascetics has increased. But now due to Beloved-of-the-Gods' Dhamma practice, the sound of the drum [for announcing the punishment of criminals] has been replaced by the sound of the Dhamma. The sighting of heavenly cars, auspicious elephants, bodies of fire, and other divine sightings has not happened for many hundreds of years. But now because Beloved-of-the-Gods, King Piyadasi, promotes restraint in the killing and harming of living beings, proper behavior towards relatives, Brahmans and ascetics, and respect for mother, father and elders, such sightings have increased.

5. In the past there were no [officers of the Dhamma] but such officers were appointed by me thirteen years after my coronation. Now they work among all religions for the establishment of Dhamma. . . . They work among soldiers, chiefs, Brahmans, householders, the poor, the aged and those devoted to Dhamma — for their welfare and happiness — so that they may be free from harassment. They . . . work for the proper treatment of prisoners, towards their unfettering. . . . They are occupied everywhere. . . .

7. Beloved-of-the-Gods, King Piyadasi, desires that all religions should reside everywhere, for all of them desire self-control and purity of heart.

8. In the past kings used to go out on pleasure tours during which there was hunting and other entertainment. But ten years after Beloved-of-the-Gods had been coronated, he went on a tour to Sambodhi [the site of the Buddha's enlightenment] and thus instituted Dhamma tours. During these tours, the following things took place: visits and gifts to Brahmans and ascetics, visits and gifts of gold to the aged, visits to people in the countryside, instructing them in Dhamma. . . .

12. Beloved-of-the-Gods, King Piyadasi, honors both ascetics and the householders of all religions, and he honors them with gifts and honors of various kinds. . . . Whoever praises his own religion, due to excessive devotion, and condemns others with the thought "Let me glorify my own religion," only harms his own religion. Therefore contact [between religions] is good. One should listen to and respect the doctrines professed by others.

Source: *The Edicts of King Ashoka,* translated by Ven S. Dhammika (Kandy, Sri Lanka: Buddhist Publication Society, 1993). Reprinted by permission of the Buddhist Publication Society.

ESSAY QUESTIONS

Political Authority in Second-Wave Civilizations

1. **Making comparisons:** How would you describe the range of political thinking and practice expressed in these sources? What, if any, common elements do they share? Another approach to such a comparison is to take the ideas expressed in one source and ask how they might be viewed by several of the others. For example, how might Darius (who commissioned the Behistun Inscription), Pericles, or Han Fei have responded to Ashoka? How might Augustus, Darius, or Athenian leaders have responded to the funerary complex of Qin Shihuangdi and the political ideology it represented?

2. **Comparing ancient and modern politics:** What enduring issues of political life do these sources raise? What elements of political thinking and practice during the second-wave era differ most sharply from those of the modern world of the last century or two? What are the points of similarity?

3. **Distinguishing "power" and "authority":** "Power" refers to the ability of rulers to coerce their subjects into some required behavior, while "authority" denotes the ability of those rulers to persuade their subjects to obey voluntarily by convincing them that it is proper, right, or natural to do so. What appeals to "power" and "authority" can you find in these sources? How does the balance between them differ among these documents?

4. **Noticing point of view:** From what position and with what motivation did these writers compose their documents? How did this affect what they had to say?

5. **Considering religion and political life:** To what extent and in what ways did religion underlie political authority in the civilizations of the second-wave era?

Notes

1. Paul Zanker, *The Power of Images in the Age of Augustus* (Ann Arbor: University of Michigan Press, 1988), 187.

2. Quoted in Audrey Ronning Topping, "China's Incredible Find," *National Geographic*, April 1978, 448.

3. Jane Portal, *Terra Cotta Warriors: Guardians of China's First Emperor* (Washington, DC: National Geographic Society, 2008), 11.

CHAPTER 4

THINKING THROUGH SOURCES

The "Good Life" in Asian Cultural Traditions

Many of the wisdom traditions of the second-wave era were fundamentally religious, focusing on human interaction with an unseen realm. Sometimes they expressed this realm as a world of divine beings, God or gods, as in Judaism, Christianity, and some forms of Hinduism and Buddhism. Alternatively, the more mystical expressions of these faiths, as well as Chinese Daoism, at times articulated the unseen realm in less personal ways, as a sustaining or pervasive Presence, located variously above, beyond, beneath, or within the human and visible realm. Some of these traditions, Chinese Confucianism and Greek rationalism, for example, were less overtly religious, expressed in more philosophical, humanistic, or rational terms. But what they all shared was an impulse to address the moral and social implications of their understandings of the cosmos, probing the nature of a "good life" for an individual person or a "good society" for a community of people. How should we live in this world? This was among the central questions that have occupied human beings since the beginning of conscious thought. And that question certainly played a major role in the emerging cultural traditions of the second-wave civilizations all across Eurasia. The sources that follow present a sample of this thinking drawn from Chinese, Indian, and Middle Eastern traditions.

Source 4.1
Reflections from Confucius

No one was more central to the making of Chinese civilization than Confucius (551–479 B.C.E.). In the several generations following their master's death, his disciples recalled his teachings and his conversations, recording them in a small book called the *Analects*. This text became a touchstone for all educated people in China and across much of East Asia as well. Over the centuries, extensive commentaries and interpretations of Confucius's teachings gave rise to a body of literature known generally as Confucianism, though these ideas encompassed the thinking of many others as well.

In the translation from the *Analects* that follows, the word "virtue" refers to the qualities of a complete or realized human being, sometimes rendered in Confucian literature as a "gentleman" or a "virtuous man." The terms "propriety" and "rites of propriety" point to an elaborate set of rituals or expectations that defined appropriate behavior in virtually every circumstance of life, depending on one's gender, age, or class.

Questions to consider as you examine the source:

- How would Confucius characterize such a fully developed person? How might one become this kind of person?

- What is "filial piety," and why is it so important in Confucius's understanding of a good society?

- How do "virtue," "filial piety," and "learning" relate to the larger task of creating good government and a harmonious society? What is Confucius's understanding of the "good life" and how it might be generated?

CONFUCIUS

The Analects
ca. 479–221 B.C.E.

The philosopher Yu said, "They are few who, being filial and fraternal, are fond of offending against their superiors. There have been none, who, not liking to offend against their superiors, have been fond of stirring up confusion. . . ."

The Master said, "To rule a country of a thousand chariots, there must be reverent attention to business, and sincerity; economy in expenditure, and love for men; and the employment of the people at the proper seasons."

The Master said, "A youth, when at home, should be filial, and, abroad, respectful to his elders. He should be earnest and truthful. He should over-flow in love to all, and cultivate the friendship of the good. When he has time and opportunity, after the performance of these things, he should employ them in polite studies."

Tsze-hsia said, "If a man withdraws his mind from the love of [beautiful women], and applies it as sincerely to the love of the virtuous; if, in serving his parents, he can exert his utmost strength; if, in serving his prince, he can devote his life; if, in his intercourse with his friends, his words are sincere: although men say that he has not learned, I will certainly say that he has."

The philosopher Tsang said, "Let there be a careful attention to perform the funeral rites to parents, and let them be followed when long gone with the ceremonies of sacrifice; then the virtue of the people will resume its proper excellence."

The Master said, "He who exercises government by means of his virtue may be compared to the north polar star, which keeps its place and all the stars turn toward it."

The Master said, "If the people be led by laws, and uniformity sought to be given them by punishments, they will try to avoid the punishment, but have no sense of shame. If they be led by virtue, and uniformity sought to be given them by the rules of propriety, they will have the sense of shame, and moreover will become good."

The Duke Ai asked, saying, "What should be done in order to secure the submission of the people?" Confucius replied, "Advance the upright and set aside the crooked, then the people will submit. Advance the crooked and set aside the upright, then the people will not submit."

Chi K'ang asked how to cause the people to reverence their ruler, to be faithful to him. . . . The Master said, "Let him preside over them with gravity; then they will reverence him. Let him be filial and kind to all; then they will be faithful to him. Let him advance the good and teach the incompetent; then they will eagerly seek to be virtuous."

The Master said, "If the will be set on virtue, there will be no practice of wickedness."

The Master said, "Riches and honors are what men desire. If they cannot be obtained in the proper way, they should not be held. Poverty and meanness are what men dislike. If they cannot be avoided in the proper way, they should not be avoided."

The Master said, "In serving his parents, a son may remonstrate with them, but gently; when he sees that they do not incline to follow his advice, he shows an increased degree of reverence, but does not abandon his purpose; and should they punish him, he does not allow himself to murmur."

Fan Ch'ih asked what constituted wisdom. The Master said, "To give one's self earnestly to the duties due to men, and, while respecting spiritual beings, to keep aloof from them, may be called wisdom."

The Master said, "The superior man, extensively studying all learning, and keeping himself under the restraint of the rules of propriety, may thus likewise not overstep what is right."

The Master's frequent themes of discourse were the Odes, the History, and the maintenance of the Rules of Propriety. On all these he frequently discoursed.

The Master was wishing to go and live among the nine wild tribes of the east. Some one said, "They are rude. How can you do such a thing?" The Master said, "If a superior man dwelt among them, what rudeness would there be?"

Chi Lu asked about serving the spirits of the dead. The Master said, "While you are not able to serve men, how can you serve their spirits?" Chi Lu added, "I venture to ask about death?" He was answered, "While you do not know life, how can you know about death?"

Yen Yuan asked about perfect virtue. The Master said, "To subdue one's self and return to propriety, is perfect virtue. If a man can for one day subdue himself and return to propriety, all under heaven will ascribe perfect virtue to him."

Chung-kung asked about perfect virtue. The Master said, "It is, when you go abroad, to behave to every one as if you were receiving a great guest; to employ the people as if you were assisting at a great sacrifice; not to do to others as you would not wish done to yourself; to have no murmuring against you in the country, and none in the family."

Chi K'ang asked Confucius about government. Confucius replied, "To govern means to rectify. If you lead on the people with correctness, who will dare not to be correct?"

Truly, if the ruler is not a ruler, the subject not a subject, the father not a father, the son not a son, then even if there be grain, would I get to eat it?

The Master said, "Of all people, girls and servants are the most difficult to behave to. If you are familiar with them, they lose their humility. If you maintain a reserve toward them, they are discontented."

Source: Confucius, *The Analects*, translated by James Legge (1893).

Source 4.2
Filial Piety Illustrated

Central to the Confucian understanding of a good life and a good society was the notion of "filial piety." It was a concept that defined relationships between social inferiors and superiors, beginning in the family and extending to the larger arena of state and society. *The Classic of Filial Piety*, composed around 200 B.C.E., gave this fundamental Chinese value an enduring expression. "Our body, skin, and hair are all received from our parents," the text declared. "We dare not injure them. This is the first priority in filial duty. To establish oneself in the world and practice the Way; to uphold one's good name for posterity and give glory to one's father and mother — this is the completion of filial duty. Thus filiality begins with service to parents, continues in service to the ruler, and ends with establishing oneself in the world [and becoming an exemplary person]."[1] Reissued many times over many centuries, this text was accompanied by images illustrating the concept. Source 4.2 is an example of one such image, showing a good son and his wife honoring the son's parents, while two children at the bottom right observe the scene.

Questions to consider as you examine the source:

- How is the son expressing filial piety?
- What is the small child on the bottom right learning from this experience?
- How might you interpret the demeanor of the seated parents?

Filial Piety

National Palace Museum, Taipei, Taiwan/The Art Archive at Art Resource, NY

Source 4.3
A Daoist Perspective on the Good Life

Chinese thinking about the good life was not limited to the Confucian tradition. An alternative to it took shape in the writings of the mysterious figure of Laozi, who, it is said, chose to pursue the Way (*dao*) beyond the confines of Chinese civilization. The tradition that arose from Laozi and those who expanded on his ideas became known as Daoism. Here are brief selections from Laozi's famous work, the *Daodejing* (*The Way and Its Power*), which emerged around 500 B.C.E.

Questions to consider as you examine the source:

■ How does Laozi's prescription for a good life differ from that of Confucius?

■ How do you understand the concept of *wu-wei* or non-action?

■ To what does the concept of *dao* refer? What role does it play in Laozi's understanding of a good life?

Laozi

Daodejing

500 B.C.E.

1. The Dao that can be told of is not the eternal Dao. The name that can be named is not the eternal name. The Nameless is the origin of Heaven and Earth. The Named is the mother of all things.

2. [T]he sage manages affairs without action [*wu-wei*] and spreads doctrines without words. All things arise, and he does not turn away from them. He produces them, but does not take possession of them. He acts, but does not rely on his own ability. He accomplishes his task, but does not claim credit for it. It is precisely because he does not claim credit that his accomplishment remains with him.

3. Do not exalt the worthy, so that the people shall not compete. Do not value goods that are hard to get, so that the people shall not steal. Do not display objects of desire, so that the people's hearts shall not be disturbed. Therefore in the government of the sage, he keeps their hearts vacuous, fills their bellies, weakens their ambitions, and strengthens their bones. He always causes his people to be without knowledge or desire, and the crafty to be afraid to act. By acting without action, all things will be in order.

8. The best man is like water. Water is good; it benefits all things and does not compete with them. It dwells in lowly places that all disdain. This is why it is so near to the Dao. The best man in his dwelling loves the earth. In his heart, he loves what is profound. In his associations, he loves humanity. In his words, he loves faithfulness. In government, he loves order. In handling affairs, he loves competence. In his activities, he loves timeliness.

11. Thirty spokes are united around the hub to make a wheel, but it is on its non-being [emptiness, absence] that the utility of the carriage depends. Clay is molded to form a utensil, but it is on its non-being that the utility of the utensil depends. Doors and windows are cut out to make a room, but it is on its non-being that the utility of the room depends. Therefore turn being into advantage, and turn non-being into utility.

17. The best rulers are those whose existence is merely known by the people. The next best are those who are loved and praised. The next are those who are feared. And the next are those who are despised. It is only when one does not have enough faith in others that others will have no faith in him.

18. When the great Dao declined, the doctrines of humanity and righteousness arose. When knowledge and wisdom appeared, there emerged great hypocrisy. When the six family relationships are not in harmony, there will be the advocacy of filial piety and deep love to children. When a country is in disorder, there will be praise of loyal ministers.

48. The pursuit of learning is to increase day after day. The pursuit of the Dao is to decrease day after day. It is to decrease and further decrease until one reaches the point of taking no action. No action is undertaken, and yet nothing is left undone. An empire is often brought to order by having no activity. If one likes to undertake activity, he is not qualified to govern the empire.

80. Let there be a small country with few people. Let there be ten times and a hundred times as many utensils, but let them not be used. Let the people value their lives highly and not migrate far. Even if there are ships and carriages, none will ride in them. Even if there are armor and weapons, none will display them. Let the people again knot cords and use them [in place of writing]. Let them relish their food, beautify their clothing, be content with their homes, and delight in their customs. Though neighboring communities overlook one another, and the crowing of cocks and barking of dogs can be heard, yet the people there may grow old and die without ever visiting one another.

Source: Wing-tsit Ch'an, trans. *The Way of Lao Tzu* (1963).

Source 4.4
Reflections from the Hindu Scriptures

The flavor of Indian thinking about the good life and the good society is quite different from that of Confucius. This distinctive outlook is reflected in these selections from the Bhagavad Gita (The Song of the Lord), perhaps the most treasured of Hindu writings. Its dating is highly uncertain, although most scholars put it somewhere between the fifth and second centuries B.C.E. The Bhagavad Gita itself is an episode within the *Mahabharata*, one of the huge epic poems of India's classical tradition, which describes the struggle for power between two branches of the same family. The Bhagavad Gita takes place on the eve of a great battle, when the fearless warrior Arjuna is overcome with the realization that in this battle he will be required to kill some of his own kinsmen. In his distress, he turns for advice to his charioteer, Lord Krishna, who is an incarnation of the great god Vishnu. Krishna's response to Arjuna's anguished questions, a part of which is reproduced here, conveys the essence of Hindu thinking about life and action in this world. A central question in the Bhagavad Gita is how a person can achieve spiritual fulfillment while remaining active in the world.

Questions to consider as you examine the source:

■ What reasons does Krishna give for urging Arjuna to perform his duty as a warrior?

■ How does Krishna describe the good society and a fulfilled or realized individual?

■ How does this text differ from the *Analects* of Confucius? Are these texts asking the same questions? Is the Bhagavad Gita more similar to the *Daodejing*?

Bhagavad Gita
ca. Fifth to Second Century B.C.E.

The deity said, you have grieved for those who deserve no grief. . . . Learned men grieve not for the living nor the dead. Never did I not exist, nor you, nor these rulers of men; nor will any one of us ever hereafter cease to be. As in this body, infancy and youth and old age come to the embodied self, so does the acquisition of another body; a sensible man is not deceived about that. The contacts of the senses . . . which produce cold and heat, pleasure and pain, are not permanent, they are ever coming and going. Bear them, O descendant of Bharata!

He who thinks it [a person's soul, or atman] to be the killer and he who thinks it to be killed, both know nothing. It kills not, [and] is not killed. It is not born, nor does it ever die, nor, having existed, does it exist no more. Unborn, everlasting, unchangeable, and primeval, it is not killed when the body is killed. . . . As a man, casting off old clothes, puts on others and new ones, so the embodied self, casting off old bodies, goes to others and new ones. . . . It is everlasting, all-pervading, stable, firm, and eternal.

It is said to be unperceived, to be unthinkable, to be unchangeable. Therefore, knowing it to be such, you ought not to grieve. . . . For to one that is born, death is certain; and to one that dies, birth is certain. . . .

Having regard to your own duty also, you ought not to falter, for there is nothing better for a Kshatriya [a member of the warrior/ruler caste] than a righteous battle. Happy those Kshatriyas, O son of Pritha! who can find such a battle . . . an open door to heaven! But if you will not fight this righteous battle, then you will have abandoned your own duty and your fame, and you will incur sin. . . .

Your business is with action alone, not by any means with fruit. Let not the fruit of action be your motive to action. Let not your attachment be fixed on inaction. Having recourse to devotion . . . perform actions, casting off all attachment, and being equable in success or ill-success; such equability is called devotion. . . . The wise who have obtained devotion cast off the fruit of action, and released from the shackles of repeated births, repair to that seat where there is no unhappiness. . . .

The man who, casting off all desires, lives free from attachments, who is free from egoism and from the feeling that this or that is mine, obtains tranquility. This, O son of Pritha! is the Brahmic state. Attaining to this, one is never deluded, and remaining in it in one's last moments, one attains the Brahmic bliss [nirvana, or merging with the divine]. . . .

I have passed through many births, O Arjuna! and you also. I know them all, but you . . . do not know them. . . . Whensoever, O descendant of Bharata! piety languishes, and impiety is in the ascendant, I create myself. I am born age after age, for the protection of the good, for the destruction of evil-doers, and the establishment of piety. . . .

The fourfold division of castes was created by me according to the appointment of qualities and duties. . . . The duties of Brahmins, Kshatriyas, and Vaisyas, and of Sudras [SOO-druhs], too . . . are distinguished according to the qualities born of nature. Tranquillity, restraint of the senses, penance, purity, forgiveness, straightforwardness, also knowledge, experience, and belief in a future world, this is the natural duty of Brahmins. Valor, glory, courage, dexterity, not slinking away from battle, gifts, exercise of lordly power, this is the natural duty of Kshatriyas. Agriculture, tending cattle, trade, this is the natural duty of Vaisyas. And the natural duty of Sudras, too, consists in service.

Every man intent on his own respective duties obtains perfection. Listen, now, how one intent on one's own duty obtains perfection. Worshipping, by the performance of his own duty, him from whom all things proceed, and by whom all this is permeated, a man obtains perfection. One's duty, though defective, is better than another's duty well performed. Performing the duty prescribed by nature, one does not incur sin. O son of Kunti! one should not abandon a natural duty though tainted with evil; for all actions are enveloped by evil, as fire by smoke.

One who is self-restrained, whose understanding is unattached everywhere, from whom affections have departed, obtains the supreme perfection of freedom from action by renunciation. Learn from me, only in brief, O son of Kunti! how one who has obtained perfection attains the Brahman, which is the highest culmination of knowledge. A man possessed of a pure understanding, controlling his self by courage, discarding sound and other objects of sense, casting off affection and aversion, who frequents clean places, who eats little, whose speech, body, and mind are restrained, who is always intent on meditation and mental abstraction, and has recourse to unconcern, who, abandoning egoism, stubbornness, arrogance, desire, anger, and all belongings, has no thought that this or that is mine, and who is tranquil, becomes fit for assimilation with the Brahman.

Source: Tashinath Trimbak Teland, trans., The Bhagavad Gita, in *The Sacred Books of the East,* edited by Max Mueller (Oxford: Clarendon Press, 1879–1910), 8:43–46, 48–49, 51–52, 126–28.

Source 4.5
Reflections from Jesus

Like Confucius, Jesus apparently never wrote anything himself. His sayings and his actions were recorded in the Gospels by his followers. The Gospel of Matthew, from which this selection is taken, was composed around 80–85 C.E. For Christian people, this passage, known as the Sermon on the Mount, has long been among the most beloved of biblical texts, regarded as a guide for effective living and the core of Jesus' ethical and moral teachings. In this selection, Jesus contrasts the "broad . . . road" of conventional understanding and values with the "narrow . . . road that leads to life."

Questions to consider as you examine the source:

■ In what ways does Jesus' teaching challenge or contradict the conventional outlook of his time?

■ How would you summarize "the good life" as Jesus might have defined it?

■ How might Jesus and Confucius have responded to each other's teachings?

The Gospel of Matthew
ca. 70–100 C.E.

Now when he [Jesus] saw the crowds, he went up on a mountainside and sat down. His disciples came to him, and he began to teach them saying:

"Blessed are the poor in spirit, for theirs is the kingdom of heaven.

"Blessed are those who mourn, for they will be comforted.

"Blessed are the meek, for they will inherit the earth.

"Blessed are those who hunger and thirst for righteousness, for they will be filled.

"Blessed are the merciful, for they will be shown mercy.

"Blessed are the pure in heart, for they will see God.

"Blessed are the peacemakers, for they will be called sons of God.

"Blessed are those who are persecuted because of righteousness, for theirs is the kingdom of heaven.

"You are the salt of the earth. But if the salt loses its saltiness, how can it be made salty again? It is no longer good for anything, except to be thrown out and trampled by men.

"You are the light of the world. A city on a hill cannot be hidden. Neither do people light a lamp and put it under a bowl. Instead they put it on its stand, and it gives light to everyone in the house. In the same way, let your light shine before men, that they may see your good deeds and praise your Father in heaven.

"Do not think that I have come to abolish the Law or the Prophets; I have not come to abolish them but to fulfill them. I tell you the truth, until heaven and earth disappear, not the smallest letter, not the least stroke of a pen, will by any means disappear from the Law until everything is accomplished. Anyone who breaks one of the least of these commandments and teaches others to do the same will be called least in the kingdom of heaven, but whoever practices and teaches these commands will be called great in the kingdom of heaven. For I tell you that unless your righteousness surpasses that of the Pharisees and the teachers of the law, you will certainly not enter the kingdom of heaven.

"You have heard that it was said to the people long ago, 'Do not murder, and anyone who murders will be subject to judgment.' But I tell you that anyone who is angry with his brother will be subject to judgment. . . .

"Therefore, if you are offering your gift at the altar and there remember that your brother has something against you, leave your gift there in front of the altar. First go and be reconciled to your brother; then come and offer your gift.

"Settle matters quickly with your adversary who is taking you to court. Do it while you are still with him on the way, or he may hand you over to the judge, and the judge may hand you over to the officer, and you may be thrown into prison. I tell you the truth, you will not get out until you have paid the last penny.

"You have heard that it was said, 'Do not commit adultery.' But I tell you that anyone who looks at a woman lustfully has already committed adultery with her in his heart. . . .

"You have heard that it was said, 'Eye for eye, and tooth for tooth.' But I tell you, Do not resist an evil person. If someone strikes you on the right cheek, turn to him the other also. And if someone wants to sue you and take your tunic, let him have your cloak as well. If someone forces you to go one mile, go with him two miles. Give to the one who asks you, and do not turn away from the one who wants to borrow from you.

"You have heard that it was said, 'Love your neighbor and hate your enemy.' But I tell you: Love your enemies and pray for those who persecute you, that you may be sons of your Father in heaven. He causes his sun to rise on the evil and the good, and sends rain on the righteous and the unrighteous. If you love those who love you, what reward will you get? Are not even the tax collectors doing that? And if you greet only your brothers, what are you doing more than others? Do not even pagans do that? Be perfect, therefore, as your heavenly Father is perfect.

"Be careful not to do your 'acts of righteousness' before men, to be seen by them. . . . So when you give to the needy, do not announce it with trumpets, as the hypocrites do in the synagogues and on the streets, to be honored by men. . . . But when you give to the needy, do not let your left hand know what your right hand is doing, so that your giving may be in secret. Then your Father, who sees what is done in secret, will reward you.

"And when you pray, do not be like the hypocrites, for they love to pray standing in the synagogues and on the street corners to be seen by men. . . . But when you pray, go into your room, close the door and pray to your Father, who is unseen. Then your Father, who sees what is done in secret, will reward you. And when you pray, do not keep on babbling like pagans, for they think they will be heard because of their many words. Do not be like them, for your Father knows what you need before you ask him. . . .

"Do not store up for yourselves treasures on earth, where moth and rust destroy, and where thieves break in and steal. But store up for yourselves treasures in heaven, where moth and rust do not destroy, and where thieves do not break in and steal. For where your treasure is, there your heart will be also. . . .

"So do not worry, saying, 'What shall we eat?' or 'What shall we drink?' or 'What shall we wear?' For the pagans run after all these things, and your heavenly Father knows that you need them. But seek first his kingdom and his righteousness, and all these things will be given to you as well. Therefore do not worry about tomorrow, for tomorrow will worry about itself. Each day has enough trouble of its own.

"Do not judge, or you too will be judged. For in the same way you judge others, you will be judged, and with the measure you use, it will be measured to you.

"Why do you look at the speck of sawdust in your brother's eye and pay no attention to the plank in your own eye? How can you say to your brother, 'Let me take the speck out of your eye,' when all the time there is a plank in your own eye? You hypocrite, first take the plank out of your own eye, and then you will see clearly to remove the speck from your brother's eye. . . .

"Ask and it will be given to you; seek and you will find; knock and the door will be opened to you. For everyone who asks receives; he who seeks finds; and to him who knocks, the door will be opened.

"Enter through the narrow gate. For wide is the gate and broad is the road that leads to destruction, and many enter through it. But small is the gate and narrow the road that leads to life, and only a few find it. . . ."

When Jesus had finished saying these things, the crowds were amazed at his teaching, because he taught as one who had authority, and not as their teachers of the law.

Source: Matthew 5–7 (New International Version).

Source 4.6
Toward "Mature Manhood"

An important element of early Christian teaching about a good life involved avoiding sin and resisting temptation. This emphasis found expression in an instructional book for monks, composed in the sixth or early seventh century C.E. by Saint John Climacus and known as the *Ladder of Divine Ascent.* Written by an ascetic monk with a reputation for great piety and wisdom, the book advised monks to renounce the world with its many temptations and vices, to nurture the corresponding virtues, and to ascend step-by-step toward union with God. A twelfth-century Byzantine painting or icon was added much later to illustrate the book. There, monks are climbing the ladder of the spiritual journey toward God but are beset by winged demons representing various sins — lust, anger, pride, lying, gluttony, avarice, slander, talkativeness, and bearing grudges, among others — which are described in Climacus's book. Some have fallen off the ladder into the mouth of a dragon, which represents Hell. Repentance, or the "unbroken remembrance of one's slightest sins" is the precondition for cultivating the virtues of meekness, forgiveness, selflessness, humility, discernment, simplicity, and many other virtues. But the journey toward "mature manhood" is difficult. "Truly perilous," Climacus wrote, "is the sea that we humble monks are crossing."

Questions to consider as you examine the source:

■ Does this image support or challenge Jesus' Sermon on the Mount in describing the journey toward human fulfillment and a good life?

■ What sources of help are available for those on the "ladder of ascent"? Notice the figures in the upper left and lower right.

■ What message might beginning monks have taken from this image?

Ladder of Divine Ascent

ESSAY QUESTIONS

The "Good Life" in Asian Cultural Traditions

1. **Placing sources in context:** In what ways were these sources reacting against the conventional wisdom of their times? How was each shaped by the social and political circumstances in which it was composed?

2. **Relating spirituality and behavior:** What is the relationship between religion, which explores the transcendent realm of the gods or the divine, and moral behavior on earth in each of these sources? How does the "good life" relate to politics?

3. **Defining the "good person":** How do each of these texts characterize the fulfilled person or the fully realized human being? How do they define personal virtue?

Note

1. Wm. Theodore de Bary and Irene Bloom, compilers, *Sources of Chinese Tradition*, 2nd ed., vol. 1 (New York: Columbia University Press, 1999), 326–29.

CHAPTER 5

THINKING THROUGH SOURCES

Patriarchy and Women's Voices

Patriarchy has been a consistent feature of all civilizations. In recent decades, it has been a subject of intense interest to historians operating within local, national, and global contexts alike. They have sought to uncover how patriarchy emerged and changed over time; how it was expressed and experienced; what mix of opportunities and limitations it has afforded to women; and how different cultural traditions defined appropriate gender roles and gender identities, both feminine and masculine. But also of interest was the issue of pushback. To what extent were some women, at least, able to resist the oppressive features of patriarchy, to take advantage of its paternalistic dimensions, and to occupy nontraditional roles in their societies?

In exploring such questions, historians face a major problem: the scarcity of sources written by women themselves, especially in the premodern era. Furthermore, most of the female-authored sources we do have derive from elite women. As a result, scholars must sometimes make careful use of documents written by men, often "reading between the lines" to discern the perspectives of women. The documents and images that follow explore various expressions of patriarchy and the women's voices that emerged within them in several of the second-wave civilizations.

Source 5.1
A Greek Expression of Patriarchy

Second-wave civilizations articulated their understanding of patriarchy in various ways. Among the Greeks, Aristotle stands out for the long-term influence of his views on women within Western civilization into the modern era. As to women's inferiority, Aristotle is clear: They are "mutilated" or "inferior" men. "[T]he male . . . is by nature more expert at leading than the female. . . . [T]he relation of male to female is by nature a relation of superior to inferior and ruler to ruled." This position of women derives from some "natural deficiency" in their capacity for reason. In this respect, according to Aristotle, women lie somewhere between slaves and children. "The slave is wholly lacking the deliberative element [reason]; the female has it but it lacks authority; the child has it but it is incomplete."[1] And so women are excluded completely from public life. Even their role in procreation is passive; they are merely the material receptacle for the active element of male sperm. In the selection that follows, Aristotle builds on these assumptions as he outlines his view of a "good wife."

Questions to consider as you examine the source:

■ What are the chief qualities of a "good wife" in Aristotle's view?

■ How do these qualities reflect his understanding of women's inherent inferiority?

■ Does Aristotle prescribe any respect, protections, or benefits for women within marriage? How might the oppression inherent in patriarchy exist alongside kindness and affection between husband and wife?

ARISTOTLE

"On a Good Wife"

ca. 330 B.C.E.

A good wife should be the mistress of her home, having under her care all that is within it, according to the rules we have laid down. She should allow none to enter without her husband's knowledge, dreading above all things the gossip of gadding women, which tends to poison the soul. She alone should have knowledge of what happens within. She must exercise control of the money spent on such festivities as her husband has approved — keeping, moreover, within the limit set by law upon expenditure, dress, and ornament — and remembering that beauty depends not on costliness of raiment. Nor does abundance of gold so conduce to the praise of a woman as self-control in all that she does. This, then, is the province over which a woman should be minded to bear an orderly rule; for it seems not fitting that a man should know all that passes within the house. But in all other matters, let it be her aim to obey her husband; giving no heed to public affairs, nor having any part in arranging the marriages of her children.

Rather, when the time shall come to give or receive in marriage sons or daughters, let her then hearken to her husband in all respects, and agreeing with him obey his wishes. It is fitting that a woman of a well-ordered life should consider that her husband's wishes are as laws appointed for her by divine will, along with the marriage state and the fortune she shares. If she endures them with patience and gentleness, she will rule her home with ease; otherwise, not so easily. Therefore not only when her husband is in prosperity and good report must she be in agreement with him, and to render him the service he wills, but also in times of adversity. If, through sickness or fault of judgment, his good fortune fails, then must she show her quality, encouraging him ever with words of cheer and yielding him obedience in all fitting ways — only let her do nothing base or unworthy. Let her refrain from all complaint, nor charge him with the wrong, but rather attribute everything of this kind to sickness or ignorance or accidental errors. . . . Therefore his wife's training should be the object of a man's unstinting care; that so far as is possible their children may spring from the noblest of stock. For it is only by this means that each mortal, successively produced, participates in immortality; and that petitions and prayers continue to be offered to ancestral gods. So that he who thinks lightly of this would seem also to be slighting the gods. For their sake then, in whose presence he offered sacrifice and led his wife home, promising to honor her far above all others saving his parents, a man must have care for wife and children.

Now a virtuous wife is best honored when she sees that her husband is faithful to her, and has no preference for another woman. . . . Therefore it befits not a man of sound mind to bestow his person promiscuously, or have random intercourse with women; for otherwise the base-born will share in the rights of his lawful children, and his wife will be robbed of her honor due, and shame be attached to his sons.

And it is fitting that he should approach his wife in honor, full of self-restraint and awe; and in his conversation with her, should use only the words of a right-minded man, suggesting only such acts as are themselves lawful and honorable. And if through ignorance she has done wrong, he should advise her of it in a courteous and modest manner. . . . And if the husband learns first to master himself, he will thereby become his wife's best guide in all the affairs of life, and will teach her to follow his example.

Source: Aristotle, *The Politics & Economics of Aristotle*, translated by Edward English Walford and John Gillies (London: G. Bell & Sons, 1908).

Source 5.2
An Indian Expression of Patriarchy

The early centuries of Indian civilization (1500–500 B.C.E.) provide evidence for a degree of independence and respect for women of the upper castes. They participated in religious rituals, composed some of the hymns in the Vedas, could sometimes freely choose their husbands, were able to move freely in public, and could remarry. Much of this changed and a far more rigid patriarchy took hold as India's classical civilization crystallized during the second-wave era. That patriarchy found expression in the Laws of Manu, a huge compilation of prescriptions for an ideal society, which developed around 200–400 C.E.

Questions to consider as you examine the source:

■ What restrictions does this text place on the lives of women?

■ What assumptions about social life and the role of women underlie these restrictions?

■ How does the tone and substance of this Indian text compare with that of Aristotle?

The Laws of Manu
200–400 C.E.

Hear now the duties of women.

By a girl, by a young woman, or even by an aged one, nothing must be done independently, even in her own house.

In childhood a female must be subject to her father, in youth to her husband, when her lord is dead to her sons; a woman must never be independent.

She must not seek to separate herself from her father, husband, or sons; by leaving them she would make both (her own and her husband's) families contemptible.

She must always be cheerful, clever in (the management of her) household affairs, careful in cleaning her utensils, and economical in expenditure.

Him to whom her father may give her, or her brother with the father's permission, she shall obey as long as he lives, and when he is dead, she must not insult (his memory). . . .

Though destitute of virtue, or seeking pleasure (elsewhere), or devoid of good qualities, (yet) a husband must be constantly worshipped as a god by a faithful wife.

No sacrifice, no vow, no fast must be performed by women apart (from their husbands); if a wife obeys her husband, she will for that (reason alone) be exalted in heaven. . . .

[S]he must never even mention the name of another man after her husband has died. . . .

By violating her duty towards her husband, a wife is disgraced in this world, (and after death) she enters the womb of a jackal, and is tormented by diseases (the punishment of) her sin. . . .

[A] female who controls her thoughts, speech, and actions, gains in this (life) highest renown, and in the next (world) a place near her husband. . . .

No man can completely guard women by force; but they can be guarded by the . . . (following) expedients: let the (husband) employ his (wife) in the collection and expenditure of his wealth, in keeping (everything) clean, in (the fulfilment of) religious duties, in the preparation of his food, and in looking after the household utensils. . . .

Through their passion for men, through their mutable temper, through their natural heartlessness, they become disloyal towards their husbands, however carefully they may be guarded in this (world).

The husband receives his wife from the gods, (he does not wed her) according to his own will; doing what is agreeable to the gods, he must always support her (while she is) faithful.

"Let mutual fidelity continue until death," — this may be considered as the summary of the highest law for husband and wife.

Source: The Laws of Manu, in *The Sacred Books of the East*, vol. 25, translated by G. Bühler (Oxford, UK: Clarendon Press, 1886), 194–97, 328–30, 332, 335, 344–45.

Source 5.3
A Chinese Woman's Instructions to Her Daughters

Strangely enough, Chinese patriarchy found its classical expression in the writing of a woman, Ban Zhao (45–116 C.E.). Confucius himself had apparently said little about women, perhaps reflecting his assumptions about their limited importance in Chinese society. Born into an elite family with connections to the imperial court, Ban Zhou received a fine literary education, was married at the age of fourteen, gave birth to several children, and was widowed early in life. In keeping with Chinese tradition, she never remarried, but she had a significant career as a court historian and as an adviser to the empress-dowager (the widow of a deceased emperor). Her most famous work, *Lessons for Women*, was an effort to apply the principles of Confucianism to the lives and behavior of women.

Questions to consider as you examine the source:

■ How would Ban Zhao define an ideal woman? An ideal man? An ideal marriage?

■ In what ways does *Lessons for Women* reflect Confucian attitudes (see Source 4.1 in the Thinking through Sources feature for Chapter 4)?

■ How might you understand Ban Zhao's work as pushing back against the limitations of Confucian patriarchy? In what ways is she critical of existing attitudes and practices regarding women?

BAN ZHAO

Lessons for Women

Late First Century C.E.

I, the unworthy writer, am unsophisticated, unenlightened, and by nature unintelligent, but I am fortunate both to have received not a little favor from my scholarly Father, and to have had a cultured mother and instructresses upon whom to rely for a literary education as well as for training in good manners. More than forty years have passed since at the age of fourteen I took up the dustpan and the broom in the Cao family [the family into which she married]. During this time with trembling heart I feared constantly that I might disgrace my parents, and that I might multiply difficulties for both the women and the men of my husband's family. Day and night I was distressed in heart, but I labored without confessing weariness. Now and hereafter, however, I know how to escape from such fears.

Being careless, and by nature stupid, I taught and trained my children without system. . . . I do grieve that you, my daughters, just now at the age for marriage, have not . . . learned the proper customs for married women. I fear that by failure in good manners in other families you will humiliate both your ancestors and your clan. . . . At hours of leisure I have composed . . . these instructions under the title, Lessons for Women.

Humility

On the third day after the birth of a girl the ancients observed three customs: first to place the baby below the bed; second to give her a potsherd [a piece of a broken pot] with which to play; and third to announce her birth to her ancestors by an offering. Now to lay the baby below the bed plainly indicated that she is lowly and weak, and should regard it as her primary duty to humble herself before others. To give her potsherds with which to play indubitably signified that she should practice labor and consider it her primary duty to be industrious. To announce her birth before her ancestors clearly meant that she ought to esteem as her primary duty the continuation of the observance of worship in the home.

These three ancient customs epitomize woman's ordinary way of life and the teachings of the traditional ceremonial rites and regulations. Let a woman modestly yield to others; let her respect others; let her put others first, herself last. . . . Always let her seem to tremble and to fear. When a woman follows such maxims as these then she may be said to humble herself before others. . . .

Let a woman retire late to bed, but rise early to duties; let her not dread tasks by day or by night. . . . When a woman follows such rules as these, then she may be said to be industrious.

Let a woman be correct in manner and upright in character in order to serve her husband. . . . Let her love not gossip and silly laughter. Let her cleanse and purify and arrange in order the wine and the food for the offerings to the ancestors. When a woman observes such principles as these, then she may be said to continue ancestral worship.

Husband and Wife

The Way of husband and wife is intimately connected with Yin and Yang and relates the individual to gods and ancestors. Truly it is the great principle of Heaven and Earth, and the great basis of human relationships. . . .

If a husband be unworthy, then he possesses nothing by which to control his wife. If a wife be unworthy, then she possesses nothing with which to serve her husband. If a husband does not control his wife, then the rules of conduct manifesting his authority are abandoned and broken. If a wife does not serve her husband, then the proper relationship between men and women and the natural order of things are neglected and destroyed. As a matter of fact the purpose of these two is the same.

Now examine the gentlemen of the present age. They only know that wives must be controlled, and that the husband's rules of conduct manifesting his authority must be established. They therefore teach their boys to read books and study histories. But they do not in the least understand that husbands and masters must also be served, and that the proper relationship and the rites should be maintained. Yet only to teach men and not to teach women — is that not ignoring the essential relation between them? According to the "Rites" [a classic text], it is the rule to begin to teach children to read at the age of eight years, and by the age of fifteen years they ought then to be ready for cultural training. Only why should it not be that girls' education as well as boys' be according to this principle?

Respect and Caution

As Yin and Yang are not of the same nature, so man and woman have different characteristics. The distinctive quality of the Yang is rigidity; the function of the Yin is yielding. Man is honored for strength; a woman is beautiful on account of her gentleness. Hence there arose the common saying: "A man though born like a wolf may, it is feared, become a weak monstrosity; a woman though born like a mouse may, it is feared, become a tiger."

Now for self-culture nothing equals respect for others. . . . Consequently it can be said that the Way of respect and acquiescence is woman's most important principle of conduct. . . . Those who are steadfast in devotion know that they should stay in their proper places. . . .

If husband and wife have the habit of staying together, never leaving one another, and following each other around within the limited space of their own rooms, then they will lust after and take liberties with one another. From such action improper language will arise between the two. This kind of discussion may lead to licentiousness. But of licentiousness will be born a heart of disrespect to the husband. Such a result comes from not knowing that one should stay in one's proper place. . . .

If wives suppress not contempt for husbands, then it follows that such wives rebuke and scold their husbands. If husbands stop not short of anger, then they are certain to beat their wives. The correct relationship between husband and wife is based upon harmony and intimacy, and conjugal love is grounded in proper union. Should actual blows be dealt, how could matrimonial relationship be preserved? Should sharp words be spoken, how could conjugal love exist? If love and proper relationship both be destroyed, then husband and wife are divided.

Womanly Qualifications

A woman ought to have four qualifications: (1) womanly virtue; (2) womanly words; (3) womanly bearing; and (4) womanly work. Now what is called womanly virtue need not be brilliant ability, exceptionally different from others. Womanly words need be neither clever in debate nor keen in conversation. Womanly appearance requires neither a pretty nor a perfect face and form. Womanly work need not be work done more skillfully than that of others.

To guard carefully her chastity; to control circumspectly her behavior; in every motion to exhibit modesty; and to model each act on the best usage, this is womanly virtue.

To choose her words with care; to avoid vulgar language; to speak at appropriate times; and not to weary others with much conversation, may be called the characteristics of womanly words.

To wash and scrub filth away; to keep clothes and ornaments fresh and clean; to wash the head and bathe the body regularly, and to keep the person free from disgraceful filth, may be called the characteristics of womanly bearing.

With whole-hearted devotion to sew and to weave; to love not gossip and silly laughter; in cleanliness and order to prepare the wine and food for serving guests, may be called the characteristics of womanly work. . . .

Implicit Obedience

Whenever the mother-in-law says, "Do not do that," and if what she says is right, unquestionably the daughter-in-law obeys. Whenever the mother-in-law says, "Do that," even if what she says is wrong, still the daughter-in-law submits unfailingly to the command. Let a woman not act contrary to the wishes and the opinions of parents-in-law about right and wrong; let her not dispute with them what is straight and what is crooked. Such docility may be called obedience which sacrifices personal opinion. Therefore the ancient book, A Pattern for Women, says: "If a daughter-in-law who follows the wishes of her parents-in-law is like an echo and shadow, how could she not be praised?"

Source: Nancy Lee Swann, trans., *Pan Chao: Foremost Woman Scholar of China* (New York: Century, 1932), 82–90. Reprinted with permission.

Source 5.4
An Alternative to Patriarchy in India

For some women in some places, religion offered a partial escape from the limitations of patriarchy. In India, one such path of release lay in becoming a Buddhist nun and entering a monastery, where women were relatively less restricted and could exercise more authority than in ordinary life. Known as *bhikkhunis*, such women composed hundreds of poems in the early centuries of Indian Buddhism. They were long recited and transmitted in an oral form and brought together in a collection known as the Psalms of the Sisters, which was set to writing probably during the first century B.C.E. These poems became part of the officially recognized Buddhist scriptures, known as the Pali Canon. As such, they represent the only early text in any of the world's major religions that was written by women and about the religious experience of women. A selection of these poems follows here.

Questions to consider as you examine the source:

■ In what ways might these poems represent a criticism of Indian patriarchy?

■ How do these poems reflect core Buddhist teachings?

■ What criticism of the women who wrote these poems would you anticipate? How might supporters of the Laws of Manu view the renunciation that these nuns practiced?

Psalms of the Sisters
First Century B.C.E.

Sumangala's Mother

O woman well set free! how free am I,
How thoroughly free from kitchen drudgery!
Me stained and squalid 'mong my cooking-pots
My brutal husband ranked as even less
Than the sunshades he sits and weaves alway.
Purged now of all my former lust and hate,
I dwell, musing at ease beneath the shade
Of spreading boughs — O, but 'tis well with me!

A Former Courtesan

How was I once puff'd up, incens'd with the bloom of
    my beauty,
Vain of my perfect form, my fame and success 'midst
    the people,
Fill'd with the pride of my youth, unknowing the
    Truth and unheeding!
Lo! I made my body, bravely arrayed, deftly painted,
Speak for me to the lads, whilst I at the door of the harlot
Stood, like a crafty hunter, weaving his snares, ever
    watchful.
Yea, I bared without shame my body and wealth of
    adorning;
Manifold wiles I wrought, devouring the virtue of many.
To-day with shaven head, wrapt in my robe,
I go forth on my daily round for food; . . .
Now all the evil bonds that fetter gods
And men are wholly rent and cut away. . . .
Calm and content I know Nibbana's Peace.

The Daughter of a Poor Brahmin

Fallen on evil days was I of yore.
No husband had I, nor no child, no friends
Or kin — whence could I food or raiment find? As
    beggars go, I took my bowl and staff,
And sought me alms, begging from house to house,
Sunburnt, frost-bitten, seven weary years.
Then came I where a woman Mendicant
Shared with me food, and drink, and welcomed me,
And said: "Come forth into our homeless life!" . . .
I heard her and I marked, and did her will.

The Daughter of a Wealthy Treasurer

Daughter of Treas'rer Majjha's famous house,
Rich, beautiful and prosperous, I was born
To vast possessions and to lofty rank.
Nor lacked I suitors — many came and wooed;
The sons of Kings and merchant princes came
With costly gifts, all eager for my hand. . . .
But I had seen th' Enlightened, Chief o' the World,
    The One Supreme [the Buddha].
And [I] knew this world should see me ne'er return.
Then cutting off the glory of my hair,
I entered on the homeless ways of life.
'Tis now the seventh night since first all sense
Of craving drièd up within my heart.

Subhā, the Goldsmith's Daughter

A maiden I, all clad in white, once heard
The Norm [Buddhist teaching], and hearkened eager,
    earnestly,
So in me rose discernment of the Truths.
Thereat all worldly pleasures irked me sore,
For I could see the perils that beset
This reborn compound, "personality,"
And to renounce it was my sole desire.
So I forsook my world — my kinsfolk all,
My slaves, my hirelings, and my villages,
And the rich fields and meadows spread around,
Things fair and making for the joy of life —
All these I left, and sought the Sisterhood,
Turning my back upon no mean estate. . . .
See now this Subhā, standing on the Norm,
Child of a craftsman in the art of gold!
Behold! she hath attained to utter calm.

Source: Psalms of the Sisters, vol. 1 in *Psalms of the Early Buddhists*, translated by Mrs. Rhys Davids (London: Henry Frowde, Oxford University Press Warehouse, 1909), poems 21, 39, 49, 54, 70.

Source 5.5
Roman Women in Protest

On occasion, women not only wrote but also acted in the public arena. Boudica of Britain and Trung Trac of Vietnam led movements of military resistance against Roman and Chinese invaders. Perpetua of North Africa refused the counsel of her father and of Roman officials to renounce her conversion to Christianity. Aspasia associated as an equal partner with the Athenian leader Pericles and accompanied him in the elite social circles of Athens. When Roman authorities in 42 B.C.E. imposed a tax on wealthy women, a large group of these women stormed into the Forum, where one of them, Hortensia, made a passionate speech. "Why should we pay taxes when we do not participate in public offices, nor honours, nor commands, nor the whole government," she asked. "Women's sex absolves them among all mankind [from paying taxes]."[2]

A particularly well-known example of women's public action took place in Rome, well before Hortensia's protest, in the wake of the Second Punic War with Carthage in North Africa. In 218 B.C.E., the Carthaginian commander Hannibal had invaded the Italian peninsula and threatened Rome itself. In these desperate circumstances, Roman authorities passed the Oppian Law (215 B.C.E.), which restricted women's use of luxury goods so as to preserve resources for the war effort. Twenty years later (195 B.C.E.), with Rome now secure and prosperous, Roman women demanded the repeal of those laws and in the process triggered a major debate among Roman officials. That debate and the women's protest that accompanied it were chronicled early in the first century C.E. by Livy, a famous Roman historian.

Questions to consider as you examine the source:

■ How might you summarize the arguments favoring the retention of the law (Cato) and those favoring its repeal (Lucius Valerius)? To what extent did the two men actually differ in their views of women?

■ How might one of the Roman women involved in the protest have made her own case?

■ What can we learn from Livy's account about the social position of Roman women and the attitudes of Roman men?

LIVY

History of Rome

Early First Century C.E.

The law prohibited any woman from having more than a half ounce of gold, wearing fancy clothes, or riding in a carriage through city or town. The restriction on carriages extended to distances of up to a mile from the city or town and did not apply if the woman was going to a public religious ceremony. . . .

Many upper class men publicly argued for or against the law, and a crowd of men similarly divided filled the Capitol. Women blocked the streets of the city and the entrances to the Forum, asking the men who tried to enter to repeal the law on the grounds that now the Republic as a whole was flourishing and everyone's individual circumstances were getting better. Husbands were unable to use their authority, their influence, or their embarrassment at what was happening to keep their wives at home. The crowd of women grew daily, and even women from neighboring towns and villages joined them. Then they dared to approach the consuls, praetors and other magistrates and petition them. But one of the consuls, Marcus Cato, was not at all open to their requests.

Cato spoke in support of the law they were trying to repeal:

Citizens, if each of us had aimed to maintain a husband's rights and authority over his wife, we would have less of a problem with women as a whole. Our prerogatives — already laid low in our homes by women's lack of self control — are also here in the Forum crushed and trampled. Because we did not control each woman individually, we tremble before a whole group of them. . . .

Indeed, just a little while ago I blushed red when I came into the forum through an army of women on the march. If respect for the dignity and modesty of some individual women (more than for that of the group as a whole) had not held me back. . . . I would have said, "Running around in public, blockading the streets, and accosting other women's husbands — what kind of behavior is that? Couldn't you have each individually made the same requests to your man at home? Does your charm work better in public on other women's men than it does at home on your own man? But it is not proper even at home to concern yourself with what laws should be proposed or repealed here in the Forum — at least not if the rules of modesty keep married women within proper limits."

Our ancestors did not want females to conduct any, not even personal, business without a guardian as their agent. Our ancestors wanted them to be under the control of their fathers, brothers or husbands. We, gods help us, now even allow them to engage in public affairs, and to meddle with our assemblies, voting and business in the forum. For what else are they doing now in the streets and on the corners but supporting the proposal of the people's tribunes and recommending that the law be repealed? Go ahead, give free reins to these untamed creatures with their uncontrolled natures and hope that they will put a limit to their license even if you won't. This issue is the least of what women must do against their will because of our laws and customs. They want freedom — no, to speak truthfully, license — in everything. What will they try if they triumph now? . . . The instant they begin to be your equals, they will become your superiors. . . .

What excuse can women honestly give for their rebellion? One says, "So that we can shine dressed in purple and gold, so that we can ride carriages through the city whether there is a religious festival or not." . . .

A woman who has her own money will spend it, and one who does not will ask her husband for it. Whether he gives her his money or watches her get it from another man, he will be miserable either way. But right now they solicit other women's husbands in public and, even worse, propose legislation and solicit votes — and some men are giving them what they want. . . .

Do not think, citizens, that the situation will ever be the same as it once was after the law has been repealed. . . .

Then Lucius Valerius spoke on behalf of his proposal.

. . . The women have in public petitioned you to repeal — at a time of peace when the republic is blessed and flourishing — a law passed during hard times when we were at war. And because of that, Cato calls this gathering an "insurrection" and, at times, a "women's revolt." . . . In the end, are women doing anything strange when they gather together and stand up in public on an issue that affects them? Have they never appeared in public before now? . . . Learn how often women have acted in public, and, indeed, always for the public good.

Already at the beginnings of Rome, when Romulus was king, the Sabines captured the Capitol. There was hand-to-hand combat in the Forum. Did not the women then put an end to the fight when they rushed between the two armies? . . . When the Gauls captured Rome, did not the women all together provide their gold for public use to ransom the city? And — so I do not just select examples from times past — during the most recent war with Carthage, we had a shortage of money. Did not the widows then give their money to support the pubic treasury? When we summoned new gods to aid us in those troubled times, did not the women as a whole go down to the sea to welcome the goddess Cybele? You say these cases are different. My job is not to show they are the same. It is enough to defend the women against the charge that what they are doing is not normal. Given that it is no wonder that women take action in situations affecting everyone, male and female, equally, why would we be surprised that they take action on behalf of a cause that is their very own? . . . [W]e have proud ears if, even though masters do not get upset at the requests of their slaves, we are offended by what respectable women ask of us. . . .

Who then does not know that this law is recent, passed twenty years ago when Quintus Fabius and Titus Sempronius were consuls? Since women have lived the most moral lives for years without it, what ultimately is the danger that they would rush into extravagant luxury once the law has been repealed? . . . Will the fruits of peace and public calm come to everyone but our wives? . . . And, although you, a man, can wear purple, you will not allow the mother of your children to wear a purple cloak? And will your horse's apparel be more splendid than your wife's? . . .

Cato said that there would be no rivalry between individual women if they owned nothing. But, by Hercules, there is universal pain and anger when they cannot wear jewelry yet see the wives of our Latin allies do so, when they see them conspicuous in gold and purple, when they see them ride through the city and have to follow them on foot, as if we did not rule over the Latin cities. Such things can wound men's spirits. What do you think they do to our little gals? Even minor things bother them. Women cannot be magistrates or priests, hold a triumph, receive honors, rewards, or get the spoils of war. Elegance, fancy dress and refinement — these are their honors. They rejoice and glory in them. Our ancestors called these things "the women's world." What else besides purple and gold do women take off while mourning? What else do they put on when done with mourning? What do they do for religious festivals and thanksgivings except wear fancier dress?

"If you repeal the Oppian law, you will not have the authority to forbid any of the things which the law forbids. Some men will have less control of their daughters, wives and sisters." Really? Women always want to be slaves to their male relatives and husbands. And they themselves hate the freedom that comes from the death of a husband or male relatives. They prefer that you, instead of a law, decide how they dress. And you should act as their guardians and keep them in hand, but not in slavery. Prefer to be called fathers or husbands, not masters.

The consul just now used prejudicial terms when he called this a "women's revolt" and an "insurrection." For the danger, supposedly, is that they will seize the Sacred Mount . . . as the lower classes once did when they were angry. But women in their weakness must live with whatever you decide, and the more powerful your authority, the more you should use it in moderation.

After these speeches for and against the law, a much larger crowd of women poured forth in public the next day. Like an army they lay siege to the houses of Marcus and Publius Brutus, the tribunes who were vetoing their colleagues' proposal to repeal the law. The women did not stand down until the tribunes withdrew their veto. . . . Twenty years after the law was passed, it was repealed.

Source: Livy, *Ab Urbe Condita*, vol. 5, books 31–35, edited by Alexander Hugh McDonald (Oxford: Oxford University Press, 1965). Translated by Edward Gutting.

ESSAY QUESTIONS

Patriarchy and Women's Voices

1. **Evaluating the possibilities of action for women:** In what ways were women able to challenge at least some elements of their societies? Do these documents exhibit anything similar to the feminist thinking or action of our own times?

2. **Internalizing social values:** To what extent did women in these civilizations internalize or accept the patriarchal values of their societies? Why might they have done so?

3. **Making judgments:** If you were a woman living during these times, which of these civilizations would you prefer to live in, and why? Do you think this kind of question — judging the past by the standards of the present — is a valid approach to historical inquiry?

Notes

1. *Internet Encyclopedia of Philosophy*, s.v. "Aristotle: Politics," by Edward Clayton, accessed May 19, 2015, http://www.iep.utm.edu/aris-pol/#SH7e.

2. Ian Michael Plant, ed., *Women Writers of Ancient Greece and Rome* (London: Equinox Publishing, 2004), 105.

CHAPTER 6

THINKING THROUGH SOURCES

Art and the Maya Elite

"The ancient Maya world," writes a major scholar of the region, "was a world of Maya art."[1] In magnificent architecture, carvings, pottery, ceramic figures, wall paintings, and illustrated books, Maya culture was suffused by a distinctive style of artistic expression — more complex, subtle, extensive, and innovative than any other in the Americas. Commissioned by Maya rulers, that art centered on life at court, depicting kings, nobles, warriors, and wealthy merchants together with the women, musicians, and artists who served them. The many deities who populated the Maya universe also appeared frequently in Maya art, which represents a major source for historians studying that civilization. While the Maya had writing, their literature was less extensive than that of Eurasian cultures, and much of it was tragically destroyed during the early decades of Spanish rule. The images that follow provide a window into the life of the Maya elite during its classical era.

Source 6.1
Shield Jaguar and Lady Xok, a Royal Couple of Yaxchilan

Carved in 724 C.E., Source 6.1 shows a royal couple from the Maya city of Yaxchilan preparing for a ceremony. According to the Maya glyphs (written symbols) in the T-shaped frame at the top of the image, the male figure on the left is King Shield Jaguar. We also know that the female figure on the right is his primary wife, Lady Xok, because the carving was located in a temple associated with her. In helping him dress for a war-related ceremony or sacrifice, Lady Xok offers her husband his helmet, the head of a jaguar, an animal that was widely associated with strength, bravery, aggression, warfare, and high social status. The king is wearing cotton body armor and carrying a knife, while his wife is clad in a huipil, a blouse similar to those still worn by Maya women in southern Mexico.

Questions to consider as you examine the source:

■ What elements of the figures' dress and decoration serve to mark their high status?

■ What might you infer about the relationship of Shield Jaguar and Lady Xok from this carving? Notice the relatively equal size of the two figures and the gesture that Shield Jaguar makes with his left hand.

Shield Jaguar and Lady Xok, a Royal Couple of Yaxchilan

National Museum of Anthropology, Mexico/Werner Forman Archive/Bridgeman Images

Source 6.2
The Presentation of Captives

Warfare was frequent among Maya cities and thus a common theme in court art. Fought with spear throwers, lances, clubs, axes, swords, and shields, Maya wars were depicted as chaotic affairs aimed at the capture of individual prisoners, who were destined for sacrifice or slavery. These prisoners were often named in the glyphs that accompanied the portrayal of battles along with the inscription "He is seized/roped."

Source 6.2, a reconstructed image, comes from a Maya archeological site in southern Mexico called Bonampak (BOHN-uhm-PAHK), well known for its vivid murals. Depicting events that took place in 792 C.E., this mural shows King Chan Muwan of Bonampak (in the center) holding a staff and receiving nine prisoners of war from his victorious noble warriors. To the right of the king in this painting are two allies from the nearby city of Yaxchilan, followed by the king's wife, his mother, and a servant-musician playing a conch. To the king's left are six more high-ranking warriors from Bonampak, while lower-level warriors guard each side of the door at the bottom.

The prisoners hold center stage in the mural. The blood flowing from several of the captives' fingers indicates that they are participating, almost certainly involuntarily, in a bloodletting ritual, while the prisoner on the far left is in the process of having his fingers cut or severed for the same purpose. Notice also the dead captive sprawling below the king's staff as a severed head lies on a bed of leaves below him. The four small images at the top indicate constellations, showing the favorable configuration of the sky for this occasion. The turtle on the far right, for example, depicts the constellation Gemini, while the three stars on its back represent what we know as Orion's Belt.

Questions to consider as you examine the source:

■ What can you infer about Maya warfare and court practice from this mural?

■ What status distinctions can you observe among the figures in the mural? Notice the jaguar skins worn by the king and three other warriors.

■ What meaning might you attach to the presence of the king's wife and mother at this event?

The Presentation of Captives

Source 6.3
A Bloodletting Ritual

The bleeding and ultimately the sacrifice of the captives in Source 6.2 was part of a more pervasive practice of bloodletting that permeated Maya religious and court life. Significant occasions — such as birth, marriage, death, planting crops, and dedicating buildings — were sanctified with human blood, the most valued and holy substance in the world. Behind this practice lay the Maya belief in the mutual relationship of humans and their gods. Two of the major scholars in this field explain: "The earth and its creatures were created through a sacrificial act of the gods, and human beings, in turn, were required to strengthen and nourish the gods."[2] The means of doing so was blood. The massive loss of blood often triggered a trancelike state that the Maya experienced as mystical union with their gods or ancestors. The lancets used to draw blood — usually from the tongue in women and often from the penis in men — were invested with sacred power.

Kings and their wives were central to this bloodletting ritual, as Source 6.3 so vividly shows. Here we meet again Shield Jaguar and Lady Xok, depicted also in Source 6.1. The date of this carving is October 28, 709 C.E. The king is holding a large torch, suggesting that the ritual occurs at night, while his kneeling wife draws a thorn-studded rope through her perforated tongue. The rope falls into a basket of bloody paper, which will be burned with the resulting smoke nourishing the gods. Shield Jaguar too will soon let his own blood flow, for the glyphs accompanying this carving declare that "he is letting blood" and "she is letting blood."

Questions to consider as you examine the source:

■ What details can you notice in the exquisitely carved work?

■ What significance might you attribute to the fact that the couple is performing this ritual together?

■ To what extent is this pervasive bloodletting a uniquely Mesoamerican religious practice? What roles do blood and sacrifice play in other religious traditions?

A Bloodletting Ritual

Lintel 24 of Yaxchilan Structure 23, from a series illustrating the accession rituals of the ruler Lord Shield Jaguar/Werner Forman Archives/Bridgeman Images

Source 6.4
The Ball Game

Among the most well-known and intriguing features of Maya life was a ball game in which teams of players, often two on a side, sought to control a rubber ball, using only their thighs, torsos, and upper arms to make it hit a marker or ring. Deeply rooted in Maya mythology, the game had long been popular throughout the Maya territory and elsewhere in Mesoamerica. On one level, it was sport, often played simply for entertainment and recreation. But the game also reflected and symbolized the prevalence of warfare among Maya cities. As one recent account put it: "The game re-enacted the paradigms for war and sacrifice, where the skillful and blessed triumph and the weak and undeserving are vanquished."[3] The ball game was yet another occasion for the shedding of blood, as losing players, often war captives, were killed, sometimes bound in ball-like fashion and rolled down the steps of the court to their death. Thus the larger mythic context of the ball game was the eternal struggle of life and death, so central to Maya religious thinking.

Source 6.4, a rollout of a vase dating from the seventh or eighth century C.E., depicts the ball game in action. Notice the heavy protective padding around the waist as well as the wrappings around one knee, foot, and upper arm of the two lead players. This equipment helped protect participants from the ball, which typically weighed seven to eight pounds. The two players on each side echo the Hero Twins of Maya mythology, famous ball players who triumphed over the lords of the underworld in an extended game and who were later transformed triumphantly into the sun and moon. The glyphs accompanying this image name two kings of adjacent cities, suggesting that the game may have been played on occasion as a substitute for warfare between rival cities.

Questions to consider as you examine the source:

- What might the elaborate dress of the players suggest about the function of the game and the status of its players?

- Notice the deer headdress on the player at the far left and the vulture image on the corresponding player at the far right. What do the headdresses suggest about the larger mythic context in which the game was understood?

- How might you compare this ancient Maya ball game to contemporary athletic contests? Consider the larger social meaning of the game as well as its more obvious features.

The Ball Game

Rollout Photograph © Justin Kerr, File no. K 2803

Source 6.5
A Maya Ruler Relaxing

Certainly not all was war, sacrifice, and bloodletting among the Maya. Source 6.5, another rollout of a vase dating from the seventh or eighth century C.E., depicts a Maya king at leisure. Attended by courtiers and musicians, whose horns and conch-shell instruments are just visible to the far left of the image, he reclines against a white cushion within easy reach of pots used to hold chocolate, a popular drink among the Maya elite, and to ferment honey into an alcoholic drink. His attention is focused on a carved dwarf figure holding a mirror. Mirrors were often consulted as oracles by Maya rulers. Many of the glyphs above this scene have yet to be deciphered by experts, although scholars have established from the inscriptions that he ruled over Motul de San José in modern Guatemala.

Questions to consider as you examine the source:

■ What does this image tell us about how Maya kings relaxed?

■ How would you describe the dress of the ruler and his courtiers in this image as compared to other depictions of kings and their entourages in this collection?

Maya King at Leisure

Rollout Photograph © Justin Kerr, File no. K 1453

ESSAY QUESTIONS

Art and the Maya Elite

1. **Considering art as evidence:** What are the strengths and limitations of art as a source of evidence? What other kinds of evidence would you want to discover to further your understanding of the Maya elite?

2. **Assessing gender roles:** In what ways are women and men depicted in these sources? What might this suggest about their respective roles in the elite circles of Maya society?

3. **Making comparisons:** How might you compare the life of the Maya elite depicted in these visual sources with that of the Roman elite of Pompeii shown in the Working with Evidence feature in Chapter 5? For a second comparison, consider the similarities and differences of Maya and Axumite civilizations.

4. **Considering the values of the historian:** What feelings or judgments do these visual sources evoke in you? Which of your values might get in the way of a sympathetic understanding of the Maya elite?

Notes

1. Mary Ellen Miller, *Maya Art and Architecture* (London: Thames and Hudson, 1999), 8–11.

2. Linda Schele and Mary Ellen Miller, *The Blood of Kings* (London: Thames and Hudson, 1992), 176.

3. Mary Miller and Simon Martin, *Courtly Art of the Ancient Maya* (New York: Thames and Hudson, 2004), 63.

THINKING THROUGH SOURCES

Life and Travel on the Silk Roads

Merchants, mercenaries, monks, and missionaries were among the prominent sojourners who traversed the Silk Roads from China to Europe, traveling much of the time in Central or Inner Asia. Many more people, of course, lived permanently or for long periods of time in the area. Hailing from an immense variety of cultures, both travelers and permanent residents contributed to turning this vast region into a vital Eurasian arena of exchange. Perhaps most obviously, it was a commercial crossroads that featured trade in numerous goods, originating from the agricultural civilizations, pastoral societies, and gathering and hunting cultures of the region. It was also a realm of cultural and religious encounters. Buddhism, Judaism, Christianity, Islam, Manichaeism (man-ih-KEE-iz'm), elements of Greek and Chinese culture — all of these traditions spread via the Silk Roads network, finding new expressions far from their places of origin. Finally, the territory encompassing the Silk Roads was an imperial crossroads, for the empires or military federations periodically established by pastoral societies clashed with the established civilizations and states of China, India, the Middle East, and Europe to the south and west.

Over the past century or so, scholars have learned much about life along the Silk Roads. Ancient manuscripts in many languages have brought to light Manichaean prayers, commercial contracts, lawsuits, medical prescriptions, erotic tales, and letters between husbands and wives. Stopping places on the trade routes, known as caravanserai, have been uncovered in oases or ancient market cities, and long-sealed caves have disclosed amazing treasures of Buddhist art. The images and documents that follow show something of life and travel on the Silk Roads and the cultural exchanges that ensued.

Among the first things that impressed travelers on the Silk Roads were the dangers from nature and man alike. Much of the route passed through harrowing terrain. Traveling from China to India in the seventh century, the Chinese Buddhist monk Xuangzang encountered mountains "so dangerously steep and tall that they seem to touch the sky." Marco Polo traversed a desert that appeared endless, where water was scarce and "birds and beasts there are none," and where sandstorms and hallucinations were a peril to travelers. Furthermore, when armies clashed or political authority broke down, human threats were added to those of nature.

Source 7.1
Dangers and Assistance on the Silk Roads

Source 7.1 shows a typical confrontation along the Silk Roads. An eighth-century painting, it was discovered in the Magao Caves near Dunhuang, a major stop on the Silk Roads and a center of Buddhist art and learning. It depicts a group of Tibetan and Central Asian merchants (on the right) who have encountered bandits or avaricious border guards (on the left). Required to unload their goods, the merchants await their fate — an extortionate payment, robbery of their goods, or maybe death. But in the Buddhist culture that pervaded much of the Silk Road network, legend had it that a wealthy merchant had gained safety during his travels by invoking the assistance of the bodhisattva Guanyin. (See Source 4.3 in the main text for a Japanese image of this Bodhisattva of Compassion.) The panel above the merchants reads in part: "If you all call upon his name, then from the malicious bandits you shall contrive to be delivered. . . . Men, by the mere calling upon his name, they shall forthwith gain deliverance."[1]

Questions to consider as you examine the source:

- What message did this painting seek to convey?

- What else might you learn about the Silk Roads from this image?

- What might have been the possible outcomes of the story that this scene describes?

Silk Road Merchants Encounter Bandits

Pictures from History/CPA Media

Source 7.2
Advice for Merchants

Given the dangers to merchants traveling the Silk Road, it is not surprising that travel guides might have a market, especially among merchants traveling the Silk Roads. One such guide was written by Francesco Pegolotti, a fourteenth-century merchant and banker from Florence with a wide range of business contacts. The following excerpts contain his advice for navigating the Silk Roads to China. Keep in mind that he was writing when the Mongol Empire provided relatively safe conditions for travel across much of the Silk Roads network.

Questions to consider as you examine the source:

- What difficulties does Pegolotti's advice anticipate?

- What recommendations does he make for dealing with these problems?

- What might historians learn about economic conditions in China at this time?

FRANCESCO PEGOLOTTI

Advice for European Merchants Traveling to China
ca. 1340

In the first place, you must let your beard grow long and not shave. And at Tana [a city on the Sea of Azov, an extension of the Black Sea] you should furnish yourself with a dragoman [interpreter]. And you must not try to save money in the matter of dragomen by taking a bad one instead of a good one. For the additional wages of the good one will not cost you so much as you will save by having him. And besides the dragoman it would be good to take at least two good manservants, who are acquainted with the Cumanian tongue [a Turkic language]. And if the merchant likes to take a woman with him from Tana, he can do so; if he does not like to take one there is no obligation, only if he does take one he will be kept much more comfortably than if he does not take one. If he does take one, it would be good if she were acquainted with the Cumanian tongue as well as the men.

And from Tana traveling to Gittarchan [Astrakhan, north of the Caspian Sea] you should take with you twenty-five days' provisions, that is to say, flour and salt fish; as for meat, you will find enough of it at all the places along the road. And also at all the chief stations [along the way] . . . , you should replenish yourself with flour and salt fish; other things you will find in sufficient quantities, especially meat.

The road you travel from Tana to Cathay [China] is perfectly safe, whether by day or by night, according to what the merchants say who have used it. But if the merchant, in going or coming, should die enroute, everything belonging to him will become the property of the lord of the country in which he dies, and the officers of the lord will take possession of all. So also if he dies in Cathay. But if his brother is with him, or an intimate friend and comrade calling himself his brother, then they will surrender the property of the deceased to this person, and so it will be rescued.

And there is another danger: this is when the lord of the country dies, and before the new lord who is to have the lordship is proclaimed. During such intervals there have sometimes been irregularities perpetrated on the Franks, and other foreigners. (They call "Franks" all the Christians of these parts from Romania [Byzantine Empire] westward.) And the roads will not be safe to travel until another lord be proclaimed who is to reign in place of him who died.

Cathay is a province that contains a multitude of cities and towns. Among others there is one in particular, that is to say the capital city, to which merchants flock, and in which there is a vast amount of trade; and this city is called Cambalec [present day Beijing, the capital of Mongol-ruled China]. And the said city has a circuit of one hundred miles, and is all full of people and houses and of dwellers in the said city. . . . You may reckon also that from Tana to Sara [a city on the Volga River] the road is less safe than on any other part of the journey; and yet even when this part of the road is at its worst, if there are some sixty men in your company you will go as safely as if you were in your own house.

Anyone from Genoa or from Venice, wishing to go to the places above-named, and to make the journey to Cathay, should carry linens with him, and if he visits Organci [on the Oxus River in Central Asia] he will dispose of these at a profit. In Organci he should purchase . . . silver, and with these he should proceed without making any further investment, unless for some bales of the very finest textiles of small bulk, and that cost no more for transportation than coarser textiles.

Merchants who travel this road can ride on horseback or on asses, or mounted in any way that they choose to be mounted.

Whatever silver the merchants might carry with them as far as Cathay the lord of Cathay will take from them and put into his treasury. And to merchants who bring silver they give that paper money of theirs in exchange. This is of yellow paper, stamped with the seal of the aforementioned lord. And this money is called *balisbi*; and with this money you can readily buy silk and all other merchandise that you desire to buy. And all the people of the country are bound to receive it. And yet you shall not pay a higher price for your goods because your money is of paper. And there are three kinds of paper money, one being worth more than another, according to the value which has been established for each by that lord.

Source: Henri Yule, ed. and trans., *Cathay and the Way Thither*, 2nd ed. (revised by H. Cordier), 4 vols. (London: Hakluyt Society, 1913–1916), 3:151–55.

Source 7.3
Stopping at a Caravanserai

If travelers faced peril on the Silk Roads, they also found places of rest and refreshment, known as caravanserai. Located periodically along the Silk Roads and often protected by powerful rulers, they provided lodging for merchants and their servants, warehouses for their goods, shelter and food for their animals in an open courtyard, medical help for the sick, and opportunities for trade in the bazaars. Source 7.3, a sixth-century painting also from the Magao Caves, shows a caravan finding accommodations in such a place. Providing these services, including wells and bridges, was one way for wealthy Buddhist patrons to gain merit.

Questions to consider as you examine the source:

■ What specific activities can you identify in the painting?

■ Which of these activities might be thought capable of generating religious merit? Notice, for example, the several figures at the bottom left of the image.

■ What additional information about the Silk Roads is apparent in this image compared to the information you can derive from Sources 7.1 and 7.2?

A Stop at a Caravanserai

Pictures from History/CPA Media

Source 7.4
Buddhism on the Silk Roads

Among the cultural traditions that spread across the Silk Roads, none was more significant than Buddhism. Buddhist monks, merchants, and missionaries traveled these roads, and the religion itself took root in the oasis cities of Central Asia and from there later spread to China, Korea, and Japan. In the two documents that follow, we catch a glimpse of life in these Central Asian Buddhist centers and their monasteries. The first derives from the oasis settlement of Niya, a commercial center on the southern route of the Silk Road at the edge of the Takla Makan Desert. Documents such as this, dating to around 300 C.E., reveal the involvement of Buddhist monks in commercial life, as they witnessed contracts and arbitrated conflicts, receiving payment in rolls of silk. They bought and sold land as well as slaves. Contrary to conventional monastic life, at least some monks in Niya also married, fathered children, and lived in their own homes. Even those who lived in the monastery participated in the local economy, much as did the ordinary residents of Niya.

Questions to consider as you examine the source:

- What tensions afflicted the life of the Niya monastery?
- Why might some monks shirk their monastic duties?
- What does this document suggest about the economic activities of the monks?

Source 7.4A
Regulations for a Community of Monks
Third Century C.E.

The community of monks in the capital laid down regulations for the community of monks in [Niya]. It is heard that novices do not pay attention to an elder; they disobey the old monks. Concerning this these regulations have been laid down by his majesty in front of the order of monks. The elders Silabrabha and Pumnasena [are to be] in charge of the monastery. They have to administer all the activities of the community. [Disputes] are to be examined in accordance with the law. . . . Whichever monk does not partake in the activities of the community of monks shall pay a fine of one roll of silk. Whichever monk does not take part in the *posatha* ceremony [a gathering of the monks to review their adherence to the rules of monastic life] his penalty is one roll of silk. Whichever monk at the invitations to the *posatha* ceremony enters in householder's dress shall pay a fine of one roll of silk. Whichever monk strikes another monk a light blow, the fine is five rolls of silk; in the case of a moderate blow, ten rolls of silk, and in the case of an excessive blow, fifteen rolls of silk.

Source: Thomas Burrow, *A Translation of the Kharoshthi Documents from Chinese Turkestan* (London Royal Asiatic Society, 1940), 95. Adapted from the Bedford series book Xinru Liu, *The Silk Roads* (Boston: Bedford/St. Martin's, 2012), 102.

Source 7.4B
FAXIAN
A Record of the Buddhist Kingdoms
ca. 416

Another Central Asian center of Buddhist life was the Kingdom of Khotan, located, like Niya, on the southern rim of the Takla Makan Desert. Enriched by the trade of the Silk Roads, Khotan flourished as a Buddhist society for a thousand years until it was overrun by Muslim armies in 1006. In the early fifth century, a Chinese Buddhist teacher named Faxian spent several months in Khotan while on his way to India and later wrote a description of what he witnessed there.

Questions to consider as you examine the source:

■ How does this account of Buddhist life on the Silk Roads compare to that of Niya?

■ What impressed Faxian about this Buddhist kingdom?

■ How do you think the wealth of the Silk Roads had changed the practice of Buddhism in Khotan and Niya?

Having been on the road for one month and five days, we reached Khotan. This is a prosperous country, and the people there are affluent. They all follow Buddhist laws and enjoy playing and listening to Buddhist music. There are tens of thousands of monks, most of whom follow Mahayana teachings. All of the monks receive food from public kitchens (and thus do not need to beg food for themselves). In this country, people's homes are not all concentrated in one location (as in most of China) but are spread out at some distance from each other, and every household is marked by its own small stupa [a tower housing relics of the Buddha]. The smallest ones are about two *zhang* [twenty feet] in height. There is a Buddhist hostel for guest monks and other travelers. . . .

The sound of a gong summons the three thousand monks to their meals. All enter the dining hall ceremonially and sit down in a designated order. The entire hall is totally in silence; even the noise made by vessels is absent. When a monk wants a servant to add more food, he does not call out to him, but raises his hand to summon him. . . .

There are fourteen large monasteries and numerous small ones in the country. On the first day of the fourth month, the people of the city start by sweeping the street and decorating its lanes [in preparation for a major festival]. . . . A four-wheeled wagon is used to support . . . the statues. . . . A statue of the Buddha stands in the wagon, attended by two bodhisattvas. Heavenly beings, carved and then enameled with golden and silver materials, are hanging above the Buddha. . . . Holding flowers and bundles of incense, the king walked barefoot to meet the Buddha. He touched the feet of the Buddha, then spread the flowers and burned the incense. . . . Every monastery provided a different, but also beautifully decorated array of wagons and statues. It took a whole day for one monastery to parade its statues.

The kings of the six states . . . give all of their precious belongings away to support Buddhism. Humans hardly ever enjoy such things themselves.

Source: *Faxian Zhuan Jiaozhu*, translated by Xinru Liu, in *The Silk Roads*, pp. 105–6. Copyright © 2012 Bedford/St. Martin's.

Source 7.5
Christianity on the Silk Roads

Buddhism was not the only religion to travel the Silk Roads. So too did Christianity, although in a much less widespread and spectacular fashion. Largely derived from the Persian-based Church of the East, this Nestorian form of Christianity had established a minor presence in Central Asia and northern China during the first millennium C.E., probably introduced by Christian missionaries and merchants following the Silk Road network. The most well-known of these initiatives occurred in 635 C.E. when the Tang dynasty emperor Taizong welcomed a Persian Christian monk named Alopen and some two dozen of his associates to the Chinese capital of Chang'an (now Xian). The Chinese court at this time was unusually open to a variety of foreign cultural traditions, including Buddhism, Islam, and Zoroastrianism in addition to Christianity.

Unlike Buddhism, Christianity did not establish a widespread or lasting presence in Central Asia or China. But for several centuries, a number of small Christian communities had flourished, generating a remarkable set of writings known as the "Jesus Sutras." (A sutra is a Buddhist religious text.) Some were carved on large stone slabs, while others were written on scrolls discovered early in the twentieth century in the caves of Dunhuang in northwestern China. What has fascinated scholars about these writings is the extent to which they cast the Christian message in distinctively Chinese terms, making use particularly of Buddhist and Daoist concepts long familiar in China. For example, at the top of a large stone tablet known as the Nestorian Monument is a Christian cross arising out of a white cloud (a characteristic Daoist symbol) and a lotus flower (an enduring Buddhist image). The written texts themselves, which refer to Christianity as the "Religion of Light from the West" or the "Luminous Religion," describe its arrival in China and outline its message within the framework of Chinese culture.

Questions to consider as you examine the source:

- How do the sutras depict the life, death, and teachings of Jesus?

- What do these texts reveal about the process of cultural blending that occurred all along the Silk Roads?

The Jesus Sutras
635–1005

The Story of Jesus

The Lord . . . sent the Cool Wind to a girl named Mo Yen. It entered her womb and . . . [she] became pregnant and gave birth to a son named Jesus, whose father is the Cool Wind. . . . [T]he Messiah . . . sought out people with bad karma and directed them to turn around and create good karma by following a wholesome path. Eventually these people, whose karma was unwholesome, formed a conspiracy against him. . . .

For the sake of all living beings and to show us that a human life is as frail as a candle flame, the Messiah gave his body to these people of unwholesome karma. For the sake of the living in this world, he gave up his life. . . .

The Four Laws of Dharma

The first law is no desire. Your heart seeks one thing after another, creating a multitude of problems. . . . Desire can sap wholesome energy. . . . This cuts us off from the roots of Peace and Joy.

The second law is no action. . . . We live our lives veering this way and that: We do things for the sake of progress and material gain, neglecting what is truly important and losing sight of the Way.

The third law is no virtue. Don't try to find pleasure by making a name for yourself through good deeds. Practice instead universal loving kindness that is directed toward everyone.

The fourth law is no truth. Don't be concerned with facts, forget about right and wrong, sinking or rising, winning or losing. Those who have awakened to the Way, who have attained the mind of Peace and Joy, who can see all karmic conditions and who share their enlightenment with others, reflect the world like a mirror, leaving no trace of themselves.

Source: Ray Riegert and Thomas Moore (eds.), *The Lost Sutras of Jesus: Unlocking the Ancient Wisdom of the Xian Monks* (Berkeley, CA: Ulysses Press, 2006), 81–83, 115, 117, 119.

Source 7.6
Letters from the Silk Roads

Some insight into the personal strains of life on the Silk Roads comes from two letters written between husband and wife, miraculously preserved and discovered during archeological excavations in the early twentieth century. The first comes from a low-ranking Chinese military official named Xuan, who wrote to his wife Yousun sometime between 103 B.C.E. and 40 C.E. Xuan had been posted to Juyan Fort on the Great Wall of China, which offered protection for Chinese merchants traveling westward on the Silk Roads. There, soldiers were assigned to particular watchtowers to be on the lookout for "barbarian" incursions. China's Han dynasty rulers also encouraged them to settle permanently in the region to establish a more solid Chinese presence at the eastern terminus of the Silk Road network.

Questions to consider as you examine the source:

■ What concerns, both personal and professional, are reflected in Xuan's letter?

■ What does this letter reveal about the policing of the Silk Roads?

Source 7.6A
From a Soldier on Guard Duty
103 B.C.E.–40 C.E.

Xuan [the husband's name] prostrate to show respect:

Yousun, my dear wife, your life is really hard. Being at the frontier in the summer, I hope you have enough food and clothing. If this is true, I feel happy at the frontier. Only because of the support of Yousun, Xuan can serve at the frontier faithfully and have no need to worry about home.

Your brother Youdu followed the county governor to arrive at Juyan on the tenth day of the month. He told me that your parents were fine. As he came here for business in a great hurry, he probably did not get a chance to see you before his departure.

On the eleventh day, I came here to report to Houguan [Xuan's superior officer]. As the work is not finished yet, I take time to write this letter, wish all my best.

I just received a letter . . . saying the station chief has arrived at the Linqu watchtower. I am writing this letter to you Yousun. The Houguan will be gone tomorrow. The inspector has not yet arrived. I had better work hard now so that I will not receive a low grade of assessment among the officers when inspected.

Source: Chen Zhi, *Juyan Hanjian Yanjiu* [Studies of the Wooden Slips from Juyan] (Tianjin: Guji Chubanshe, 1986), 492–93.

Translated by Xinru Liu. Adapted from the Bedford series book Xinru Liu, *The Silk Roads*, p. 48. Copyright © 2012 Bedford/ St. Martin's.

Source 7.6B
From an Abandoned Wife
Early Fourth Century C.E.

A second set of letters reflects the difficulties of Sogdian traders and their families on the Silk Roads. These Central Asian merchants had established a long-lasting network of exchange with China as well as settlements within China, while their language became a medium of communication along much of the Silk Roads network. One such trader, named Nanai-dhat, lived with his wife and daughter in Dunhuang on the far western edge of China during the early fourth century C.E. Amid the turmoil that followed the demise of the Han dynasty, Nanai-dhat left the area, abandoning his previously well-to-do wife Miwnay and his daughter Shayn to poverty and unwelcome service to local Chinese families. Their desperate letter to Nanai-dhat and Miwnay's letter to her mother disclose something of the personal tragedies that accompanied people far from home in times of political upheaval on the Silk Roads. Breaks in the text reflect the fragmentary remains of the letters.

Questions to consider as you examine the source:

- How do Miwnay and Shayn describe their condition? Why did they find it so humiliating?

- What had Miwnay and Shayn done to find a way back home?

- How might you explain the contrast between the greeting of the letter and its ending?

To (my) noble lord (and) husband Nanai-dhat, blessing (and) homage on bended knee, as is offered to the gods. And (it would be) a good day for him who might see you healthy, happy (and) free from illness, together with everyone; and, sir, when I hear (news of) your (good) health, I consider myself immortal!

Behold, I am living . . . badly, not well, wretchedly, and I consider myself dead. Again and again I send you a letter, (but) I do not receive a (single) letter from you, and I have become without hope towards you. My misfortune is this, (that) I have been in Dunhuang for three years thanks(?) to you, and there was a way out a first, a second, even a fifth time, (but) he refused to bring me out. I requested the leaders that support (should be given) to Farnkhund for me, so that he may take me to (my) husband and I would not be stuck in Dunhuang, (for) Farnkhund says: I am not Nanai-dhat's servant, nor do I hold his capital. I also requested thus: If he refuses to take me to (my) husband, then . . . such support for me that he may take me to (my) mother.

[*In a fragmentary section she declares that her father would not suffer her being a servant of the Chinese, before telling her husband that if his intention was for her to become a servant that*] you write to me so that I should know how to serve the Chinese. In my paternal abode I did not have such a restricted . . . as with(?) you. I obeyed your command and came to Dunhuang and I did not observe (my) mother's bidding nor (my) brothers'. Surely(?) the gods were angry with me on the day when I did your bidding! I would rather be a dog's or a pig's wife than yours!.

Sent by (your) servant Miwnay.

[*Added in the margin was a note from his daughter.*]

From (his) daughter Shayn to the noble lord Nanai-dhat, blessing (and) homage. And (it would be) a good [day] for him [who] might see [you] healthy, rested (and) happy. . . . I have become . . . and I watch over a flock of domestic animals. . . . I know that you do not lack twenty staters(?) [a unit of money] to send. It is necessary to consider the whole (matter). Farnkhund has run away; the Chinese seek him but do not find him. Because of Farnkhund's debts we have become the servants of the Chinese, I together with (my) mother.

[*In another letter Miwnay writes to her mother.*]

From her daughter, the free-woman Miwnay, to her dear [mother] Chatis, blessing and homage. . . . It would be a good day for him who might [see] you healthy and at ease; and [for me] that day would be the best when we ourselves might see you in good health. I am very anxious to see you, but have no luck. I petitioned the councillor Sagharak, but the councillor says: Here there is no other relative closer to Nanai-dhat than Artivan. And I petitioned Artivan, but he says: Farnkhund . . . And Farnkhund says: If your husband's relative does not consent that you should go back to your mother, how should I take you? Wait until . . . comes; perhaps Nanai-dhat will come. I live wretchedly, without clothing, without money; I ask for a loan, but no-one consents to give me one, so I depend on charity from the priest. He said to me: If you go, I will give you a camel, and a man should go with you, and on the way I will look after you well. May he do so for me until you send me a letter!

Source: From Professor Nicholas Sims-Williams (translator), *The Sogdian Ancient Letters,* http://depts.washington.edu/silkroad/texts/sogdlet.html. Used by permission.

ESSAY QUESTIONS

Life and Travel on the Silk Roads

1. **Defining motives:** What needs or desires inspired the economic and cultural interactions of the Silk Roads?

2. **Explaining religious change:** What do these sources suggest about the appeal of Buddhism and Christianity? How did life on the Silk Roads transform these religious traditions?

3. **Sources and perspectives:** In what ways do these sources confirm or reinforce your understanding of the Silk Roads? How do they challenge your understanding?

4. **Impressions of the Silk Roads:** Drawing on these sources, how would you describe life on the Silk Roads? What were its attractions? What made it a difficult or dangerous route?

Note

1. Jonathan Tucker, *The Silk Road: Art and History* (London: Philip Wilson, 2003), 128.

CHAPTER 8

THINKING THROUGH SOURCES

The Making of Japanese Civilization

Japan was among the new third-wave civilizations that took shape between 500 and 1500. Each of them was distinctive in particular ways, but all of them followed the general patterns of earlier civilizations in the creation of cities, states, stratified societies, patriarchies, written languages, and more. Furthermore, many of them borrowed extensively from nearby and older civilizations. In the case of Japan, that borrowing was primarily from China, its towering neighbor to the west. The sources that follow provide glimpses of a distinctive Japanese civilization in the making, even as that civilization selectively incorporated elements of Chinese thinking and practice.

Source 8.1
Japanese Political Thinking

As an early Japanese state gradually took shape in the sixth and seventh centuries, it was confronted by serious internal divisions of clan, faction, and religion. Externally, Japanese forces had been expelled from their footholds in Korea, while Japan also faced the immense power and attractiveness of a reunified China under the Sui and Tang dynasties. In these circumstances, Japanese authorities sought to strengthen their own emerging state by adopting a range of Chinese political values and practices. This Chinese influence in Japanese political thinking was particularly apparent in the so-called Seventeen Article Constitution issued by Shotoku in 604 C.E., which was a set of general guidelines for court officials.

Despite this apparent embrace of all things Chinese, Shotoku's attitude toward China itself is less clear. He inscribed various letters that he sent to the Chinese Sui dynasty ruler as follows: "The Son of Heaven of the Land of the Rising Sun to the Son of Heaven of the Land of the Setting Sun." Another read: "The Eastern Emperor Greets the Western Emperor."[1] Considering their country to be the Middle Kingdom, greatly superior to all its neighbors, Chinese court officials were incensed at these apparent assertions of equality. It is not clear whether Shotoku was deliberately claiming equivalence with China or if he was simply unaware of how such language might be viewed in China.

Questions to consider as you examine the source:

■ What elements of Confucian, Legalist, or Buddhist thinking are reflected in this document?

■ What can you infer about the internal problems that Japanese rulers faced?

■ How might Shotoku define an ideal Japanese state?

SHOTOKU

The Seventeen Article Constitution
604 C.E.

1. Harmony is to be valued, and an avoidance of wanton opposition to be honored. All men are influenced by class feelings, and there are few who are intelligent. Hence there are some who disobey their lords and fathers, or who maintain feuds with the neighboring villages. But when those above are harmonious and those below are friendly, and there is concord in the discussion of business, right views of things spontaneously gain acceptance. . . .

2. Sincerely reverence the three treasures . . . the Buddha, the Law [teachings], and the Priesthood [community of monks]. . . .

3. When you receive the Imperial commands, fail not scrupulously to obey them. The lord is Heaven, the vassal is Earth. Heaven overspreads, and Earth upbears. . . . [W]hen the superior acts, the inferior yields compliance.

4. The Ministers and functionaries should make decorous behavior their leading principle. . . . If the superiors do not behave with decorum, the inferiors are disorderly. . . .

5. Ceasing from gluttony and abandoning covetous desires, deal impartially with the [legal] suits which are submitted to you. . . .

6. Chastise that which is evil and encourage that which is good. This was the excellent rule of antiquity. . . .

7. Let every man have his own charge, and let not the spheres of duty be confused. When wise men are entrusted with office, the sound of praise arises. If unprincipled men hold office, disasters and tumults are multiplied. In this world, few are born with knowledge: wisdom is the product of earnest meditation. In all things, whether great or small, find the right man, and they will surely be well managed. . . .

10. Let us cease from wrath, and refrain from angry looks. Nor let us be resentful when others differ from us. For all men have hearts, and each heart has its own leanings. . . . [All] of us are simply ordinary men. . . .

11. Give clear appreciation to merit and demerit, and deal out to each its sure reward or punishment. In these days, reward does not attend upon merit, nor punishment upon crime. You high functionaries, who have charge of public affairs, let it be your task to make clear rewards and punishments. . . .

12. Let not the provincial authorities or the [local nobles] levy exactions on the people. In a country, there are not two lords. . . . The sovereign is the master of the people of the whole country. . . .

15. To turn away from that which is private, and to set our faces toward that which is public — this is the path of a Minister. . . .

16. Let the people be employed [in forced labor] at seasonable times. This is an ancient and excellent rule. Let them be employed, therefore, in the winter months, when they are at leisure. But from spring to autumn, when they are engaged in agriculture or with the mulberry trees, the people should not be so employed. For if they do not attend to agriculture, what will they have to eat? If they do not attend the mulberry trees, what will they do for clothing?

17. Decisions on important matters should not be made by one person alone. They should be discussed with many.

Source: W. G. Aston, trans., *Nihongi: Chronicles of Japan from the Earliest Times to A.D. 697* (London: Paul, Trench, Truebner, 1896), 2:129–33.

Source 8.2
The Uniqueness of Japan

Despite Japan's extensive cultural borrowing from abroad, or perhaps because of it, Japanese writers often stressed the unique and superior features of their own country. Nowhere is this theme echoed more clearly than in *The Chronicle of the Direct Descent of Gods and Sovereigns*, written by Kitabatake Chikafusa (1293–1354). A longtime court official and member of one branch of Japan's imperial family, Kitabatake wrote at a time of declining imperial authority in Japan, when two court centers competed in an extended "war of the courts." As an advocate for the southern court, Kitabatake sought to prove that the emperor he served was legitimate because he had descended in an unbroken line from the Age of the Gods. In making this argument, he was also a spokesman for the revival of Japan's earlier religious tradition of numerous gods and spirits, known later as Shintoism.

Questions to consider as you examine the source:

- In Kitabatake's view, what was distinctive about Japan in comparison to China and India?

- How might the use of Japan's indigenous religious tradition, especially the Sun Goddess, serve to legitimize the imperial rule of Kitabatake's family?

- How did Kitabatake understand the place of Confucianism and Buddhism in Japan and their relationship to Shinto beliefs?

KITABATAKE CHIKAFUSA

The Chronicle of the Direct Descent of Gods and Sovereigns
1339

Japan is the divine country. The heavenly ancestor it was who first laid its foundations, and the Sun Goddess left her descendants to reign over it forever and ever. This is true only of our country, and nothing similar may be found in foreign lands. That is why it is called the divine country.

In the age of the gods, Japan was known as the "ever-fruitful land of reed-covered plains and luxuriant rice fields." This name has existed since the creation of heaven and earth.... [I]t may thus be considered the prime name of Japan. It is also called the country of the great eight islands.

This name was given because eight islands were produced when the Male Deity and the Female Deity begot Japan. . . . Japan is the land of the Sun Goddess [Amaterasu]. Or it may have thus been called because it is near the place where the sun rises. . . . Thus, since Japan is a separate continent, distinct from both India and China and lying in a great ocean, it is the country where the divine illustrious imperial line has been transmitted.

The creation of heaven and earth must everywhere have been the same, for it occurred within the same universe, but the Indian, Chinese, and Japanese traditions are each different. . . .

In China, nothing positive is stated concerning the creation of the world, even though China is a country which accords special importance to the keeping of records. . . .

The beginnings of Japan in some ways resemble the Indian descriptions, telling as it does of the world's creation from the seed of the heavenly gods. However, whereas in our country the succession to the throne has followed a single undeviating line since the first divine ancestor, nothing of the kind has existed in India. After their first ruler, King People's Lord, had been chosen and raised to power by the populace, his dynasty succeeded, but in later times most of his descendants perished, and men of inferior genealogy who had powerful forces became the rulers, some of them even controlling the whole of India. China is also a country of notorious disorders. Even in ancient times, when life was simple and conduct was proper, the throne was offered to wise men, and no single lineage was established. Later, in times of disorder, men fought for control of the country. Thus some of the rulers rose from the ranks of the plebeians [commoners], and there were even some of barbarian origin who usurped power. Or some families after generations of service as ministers surpassed their princes and eventually supplanted them. There have already been thirty-six changes of dynasty since Fuxi, and unspeakable disorders have occurred.

Only in our country has the succession remained inviolate from the beginning of heaven and earth to the present. It has been maintained within a single lineage, and even when, as inevitably has happened, the succession has been transmitted collaterally, it has returned to the true line. This is due to the ever-renewed Divine Oath and makes Japan unlike all other countries. . . .

Then the Great Sun Goddess . . . sent her grandchild to the world below. . . . [The Sun Goddess] uttered these words of command: "Thou, my illustrious grandchild, proceed thither and govern the land. Go, and may prosperity attend thy dynasty, and may it, like Heaven and Earth, endure forever." . . .

Because our Great Goddess is the spirit of the sun, she illuminates with a bright virtue which is incomprehensible in all its aspects but dependable alike in the realm of the visible and invisible. All sovereigns and ministers have inherited the bright seeds of the divine light, or they are descendants of the deities who received personal instruction from the Great Goddess. Who would not stand in reverence before this fact? The highest object of all teachings, Buddhist and Confucian included, consists in realizing this fact and obeying in perfect consonance its principles. It has been the power of the dissemination of the Buddhist and Confucian texts which has spread these principles. . . . Since the reign of the Emperor Ojin, the Confucian writings have been disseminated, and since Prince Shotoku's time Buddhism has flourished in Japan. Both these men were sages incarnate, and it must have been their intention to spread a knowledge of the way of our country, in accordance with the wishes of the Great Sun Goddess.

Source: *Sources of Japanese Tradition*, Volume One, compiled by William De Bary et al. Copyright © 2001 Columbia University Press. Reprinted with permission of the publisher.

Source 8.3
Social Life at Court

For many centuries, high culture in Japan — art, music, poetry, and literature — found a home in the imperial court, where men and women of the royal family and nobility, together with various attendants, mixed and mingled. That aristocratic culture reached its high point between the ninth and twelfth centuries, but, according to one prominent scholar, it "has shaped the aesthetic and emotional life of the entire Japanese people for a millennium."[2] Women played a prominent role in that culture, both creating it and describing it. Among them was Sei Shonagon (966–1017), a lady-in-waiting to Empress Sadako. In her *Pillow Book*, a series of brief and often witty observations, Sei Shonagon described court life as well as her own likes and dislikes.

Questions to consider as you examine the source:

- What impression does Sei Shonagon convey about the relationship of men and women at court?

- How would you describe her own posture toward men, toward women, and toward ordinary people? What insight can you gain about class differences from her writing?

- In what ways does court life, as Sei Shonagon describes it, reflect Buddhist and Confucian influences, and in what ways does it depart from, and even challenge, those traditions?

SEI SHONAGON
Pillow Book
ca. 1000

That parents should bring up some beloved son of theirs to be a priest is really distressing. No doubt it is an auspicious thing to do; but unfortunately most people are convinced that a priest is as unimportant as a piece of wood, and they treat him accordingly. A priest lives poorly on meager food, and cannot even sleep without being criticized. While he is young, it is only natural that he should be curious about all sorts of things, and, if there are women about, he will probably peep in their direction (though, to be sure, with a look of aversion on his face). What is wrong about that? Yet people immediately find fault with him for even so small a lapse. . . .

A preacher ought to be good-looking. For, if we are properly to understand his worthy sentiments, we must keep our eyes on him while he speaks; should we look away, we may forget to listen. Accordingly an ugly preacher may well be the source of sin. . . .

When I make myself imagine what it is like to be one of those women who live at home, faithfully serving their husbands — women who have not a single exciting prospect in life yet who believe that they are perfectly happy — I am filled with scorn. . . .

I cannot bear men who believe that women serving in the Palace are bound to be frivolous and wicked. Yet I suppose their prejudice is understandable. After all, women at Court do not spend their time hiding modestly behind fans and screens, but walk about, looking openly at people they chance to meet. Yes, they see everyone face to face, not only ladies-in-waiting like themselves, but even Their Imperial Majesties (whose august names I hardly dare mention), High Court Nobles, senior courtiers, and other gentlemen of high rank. In the presence of such exalted personages the women in the Palace are all equally brazen, whether they be the maids of ladies-in-waiting, or the relations of Court ladies who have come to visit them, or housekeepers, or latrine-cleaners, or women who are of no more value than a roof-tile or a pebble. Small wonder that the young men regard them as immodest! Yet are the gentlemen themselves any less so? They are not exactly bashful when it comes to looking at the great people in the Palace. No, everyone at Court is much the same in this respect. . . .

Hateful Things

. . . A man who has nothing in particular to recommend him discusses all sorts of subjects at random as though he knew everything. . . .

An admirer has come on a clandestine visit, but a dog catches sight of him and starts barking. One feels like killing the beast.

One has been foolish enough to invite a man to spend the night in an unsuitable place — and then he starts snoring.

A gentleman has visited one secretly. Though he is wearing a tall, lacquered hat, he nevertheless wants no one to see him. He is so flurried, in fact, that upon leaving he bangs into something with his hat. Most hateful! . . .

A man with whom one is having an affair keeps singing the praises of some woman he used to know. Even if it is a thing of the past, this can be very annoying. How much more so if he is still seeing the woman! . . .

A good lover will behave as elegantly at dawn as at any other time. He drags himself out of bed with a look of dismay on his face. The lady urges him on: "Come, my friend, it's getting light. You don't want anyone to find you here." He gives a deep sigh, as if to say that the night has not been nearly long enough and that it is agony to leave. Once up, he does not instantly pull on his trousers. Instead he comes close to the lady and whispers whatever was left unsaid during the night. Even when he is dressed, he still lingers, vaguely pretending to be fastening his sash. . . .

Indeed, one's attachment to a man depends largely on the elegance of his leave-taking. When he jumps out of bed, scurries about the room, tightly fastens his trouser-sash, rolls up the sleeves of his Court cloak, over-robe, or hunting costume, stuffs his belongings into the breast of his robe and then briskly secures the outer sash — one really begins to hate him. . . .

It is very annoying, when one has visited Hase Temple and has retired into one's enclosure, to be disturbed by a herd of common people who come and sit outside in a row, crowded so close together that the tails of their robes fall over each other in utter disarray. I remember that once I was overcome by a great desire to go on a pilgrimage. Having made my way up the log steps, deafened by the fearful roar of the river, I hurried into my enclosure, longing to gaze upon the sacred countenance of Buddha. To my dismay I found that a throng of commoners had settled themselves directly in front of me, where they were incessantly standing up, prostrating themselves, and squatting down again. They looked like so many basket-worms as they crowded together in their hideous clothes, leaving hardly an inch of space between themselves and me. I really felt like pushing them all over sideways.

Source: *The Pillow Book of Sei Shōnagon by Sei Shōnagon* by Ivan I. Morris, Copyright © 1991 Columbia University Press. Reprinted by permission of the publisher. Republished also with permission of Oxford University Press from *The Pillow Book of Sei Shōnagon by Sei Shōnagon* by Ivan I. Morris, 1991; permission conveyed through Copyright Clearance Center, Inc., and granted by Columbia University Press.

Source 8.4
Japanese Zen Buddhism

Among Japan's imports from China, none has been received more eagerly and thoroughly than Buddhism. And among the various forms of Buddhism, none have become more Japanese than Zen, which was becoming firmly established in Japan by the twelfth and thirteenth centuries. Like all Buddhist teachings, it offered a path to the end of suffering, or to enlightenment. But for Zen practitioners, nothing external, such as deities or sacred texts, is of much help. Rather, the key practice is an inward-looking meditation, conducted under the guidance of often stern and rigorous teachers who were linked to a long lineage of transmission. In a classic formulation of Zen, there is "no dependence on words and letters; direct pointing to the mind of man; seeing into one's nature and attaining Buddhahood." In this way, individuals come to realize that they are already enlightened, that they already possess a Buddha nature. Sometimes this occurs gradually, but at other times it occurs in a flash of insight while doing something ordinary such as catching a shrimp or cutting a piece of bamboo. Thus Zen emphasized simplicity, spontaneity, and the profundity of the ordinary, and it led to compassion and tranquility, amid all the changing and difficult circumstances of life.

Zen became associated in particular with the samurai, who appreciated its emphasis on rigorous practice and intuitive action. It also informed much of Japanese secular culture, especially painting, poetry, theater, and the elaborate simplicity of the tea ceremony.

In this image by an unknown Japanese artist from the second half of the fifteenth century, something of the style and substance of Zen finds expression. With a few quick and simple brushstrokes, the artist set the scene of a story about a famous Chinese scholar-official named Su Dongpo, living in exile, caught in a sudden rainstorm, and forced to borrow a peasant's straw hat and wooden sandals. While local people laughed uproariously at the sight of a highly educated scholar in peasant attire, Su himself remained calm and unperturbed. The poetic text in the image reflected the Zen conception of "the essential oneness of all things, good and bad, whether in office or in lonely exile."[3]

Questions to consider as you examine the source:

■ What significance do you see in a Japanese Zen artist's referencing the story of a Chinese scholar?

■ What distinctive features of a Zen Buddhist outlook are expressed in this image of a solitary figure?

■ Why might members of the samurai class be attracted to such images and teachings?

Su Dongpo in Straw Hat and Wooden Shoes

Su Shi (Dongpo) in a Straw Hat and Sandals. Second half of the 15th century. Muromachi Period (1392–1573), Japan. Hanging scroll; ink on paper. Image 42¾ x 13⅛ in. (108.6 x 33.3 cm.). Overall with mounting; 74½ x 17⅝ in. (189.2 x 44.8 cm.). Overall with rollers; 74½ x 17⅞₈ x 19¾ in. (189.2 x 44.8 x 50.2 cm.). The Harry G. C. Packard Collection of Asian Art; Gift of Harry G. C. Packard; and Purchase, Fletcher, Rogers, Harris Brisbande Dick, and Louis V. Bell Funds, Joseph Pulitzer Bequest/The Metropolitan Museum of Art, New York, NY, USA/Image copyright © The Metropolitan Museum of Art/Image Source: Art Resource, NY

Source 8.5
The Way of the Warrior

As the Japanese imperial court gradually lost power to military authorities in the countryside, a further distinctive feature of Japanese civilization emerged in the celebration of martial virtues and the warrior class — the samurai — that embodied those values. From the twelfth through the mid-nineteenth century, public life and government in Japan was dominated by the samurai, while their culture and values, known as bushido, expressed the highest ideals of political leadership and of personal conduct. At least in the West, the samurai are perhaps best known for preferring death over dishonor, a posture expressed in seppuku (ritual suicide). But there was much more to bushido, for the samurai served not only as warriors but also as bureaucrats — magistrates, land managers, and provincial governors — acting on behalf of their lords (daimyo) or in service to military rulers, the shoguns. Furthermore, although bushido remained a distinctively Japanese cultural expression, it absorbed both Confucian and Buddhist values as well as those of the indigenous Shinto tradition.

The two selections that follow reflect major themes of an emerging bushido culture, the way of the warrior. The first excerpt comes from the writings of Shiba Yoshimasa (1349–1410), a feudal lord, general, and administrator as well as a noted poet, who wrote a manual of advice for the young warriors of his own lineage. Probably the man who most closely approximated in his own life the emerging ideal of a cultivated warrior was Imagawa Ryoshun (1325–1420), famous as a poet, a military commander, and a devout Buddhist. The second excerpt contains passages from a famous and highly critical letter Imagawa wrote to his adopted son (who was also his younger brother). The letter was published and republished hundreds of times and used for centuries as a primer or school text for the instruction of young samurai.

Questions to consider as you examine the source:

- Based on these accounts, how would you define the ideal samurai?

- What elements of Confucian, Buddhist, or Shinto thinking can you find in these selections? How do these writers reconcile the peaceful emphasis of Confucian and Buddhist teachings with the military dimension of bushido?

- What does the Imagawa letter suggest about the problems facing the military rulers of Japan in the early fifteenth century?

Source 8.5A
SHIBA YOSHIMASA
Advice to Young Samurai
ca. 1400

Wielders of bow and arrow should behave in a manner considerate not only of their own honor, of course, but also of the honor of their descendants. They should not bring on eternal disgrace by solicitude for their limited lives.

That being said, nevertheless to regard your one and only life as like dust or ashes and die when you shouldn't is to acquire a worthless reputation. A genuine motive would be, for example, to give up your life for the sake of the sole sovereign, or serving under the commander of the military in a time of need; these would convey an exalted name to children and descendants. Something like a strategy of the moment, whether good or bad, cannot raise the family reputation much.

Warriors should never be thoughtless or absentminded but handle all things with forethought. . . .

It is said that good warriors and good Buddhists are similarly circumspect. Whatever the matter, it is vexing for the mind not to be calm. Putting others' minds at ease too is something found only in the considerate. . . .

When you begin to think of yourself, you'll get irritated at your parents' concern and defy their instructions. Even if your parents may be stupid, if you obey their instructions, at least you won't be violating the principle of nature. What is more, eighty to ninety percent of the time what parents say makes sense for their children. It builds up in oneself to become obvious. The words of our parents we defied in irritation long ago are all essential. You should emulate even a bad parent rather than a good stranger; that's how a family culture is transmitted and comes to be known as a person's legacy. . . .

Even if one doesn't perform any religious exercises and never makes a visit to a shrine, neither deities nor buddhas will disregard a person whose mind is honest and compassionate. In particular, the Great Goddess of Ise [Amaterasu, the sun goddess], the great bodhisattva Hachiman [a Japanese deity who came to be seen as a Buddhist bodhisattva], and the deity of Kitano [patron god of learning] will dwell in the heads of people whose minds are honest, clean, and good.

———

Source: Thomas Cleary, trans. and ed., *Training the Samurai Mind* (Boston: Shambhala, 2008), 18–20.

Source 8.5B
IMAGAWA RYOSHUN
The Imagawa Letter
1412

As you do not understand the Arts of Peace [literary skills including poetry, history, philosophy, and ritual] your skill in the Arts of War [horsemanship, archery, swordsmanship] will not, in the end, achieve victory.

You like to roam about, hawking and cormorant fishing, relishing the purposelessness of taking life.

You live in luxury by fleecing the people and plundering the shrines.

ESSAY QUESTIONS

The Making of Japanese Civilization

1. **Looking for continuities:** What older patterns of Japanese thought and practice persisted despite much cultural borrowing from China? To what extent did borrowed elements of Chinese culture come to be regarded as Japanese?

2. **Noticing inconsistencies and change:** No national culture develops as a single set of ideas and practices. What inconsistencies, tensions, or differences in emphasis can you identify in these documents? What changes over time can you find in these selections?

3. **Considering Confucian reactions:** How might Confucian scholars respond to each of these documents?

Notes

1. Wm. Theodore de Bary et al., eds., *Sources of Japanese Tradition*, 2nd ed. (New York: Columbia University Press, 2001), 1:42.

2. Donald Keene, *Seeds in the Heart* (New York: Henry Holt, 1993), 477–78.

3. "Su Dongpo in Straw Hat and Wooden Shoes," *Heilbrunn Timeline of Art History*, Metropolitan Museum of Art, accessed May 26, 2015, http://www.metmuseum.org/toah/works-of-art/1975.268.39.

4. Yoshiaki Shimizu, ed., *Japan: The Shaping of Daimyo Culture, 1185–1868* (Washington, DC: National Gallery, 1988), 78.

CHAPTER 9

THINKING THROUGH SOURCES

Voices of Islam

Like all great religious traditions, Islam found expression in various forms. Its primary text, the Quran, claimed to represent the voice of the Divine, God's final revelation to humankind. Other early Islamic writings, known as hadiths, recorded the sayings and deeds of the Prophet Muhammad. Still others reflected the growing body of Islamic law, the sharia, which sought to construct a social order aligned with basic religious teachings. Devotional practices and expressions of adoration for Allah represented yet another body of Islamic literature. And beyond variations in teaching lay still further differences in the practice of Islam as it evolved in the many cultural settings in which the new religion became established. All of this gave rise to differing interpretations and contending views, generating for Islam a rich and complex tradition that has been the source of inspiration and debate for almost 1,400 years. From this immense range of expression, we present just a few samples of the voices of Islam.

Source 9.1
The Voice of Allah

To most Muslims, the Quran contains the very words of God. The Arabic term *quran* itself means "recitation," and the faithful believe that the angel Gabriel spoke God's words to Muhammad, who then recited them. Often called "noble" or "glorious," the Quran, compiled into an established text within thirty years of the Prophet's death, was regarded as a book without equal, written in the most sublime Arabic. Copying it was an act of piety, memorizing it was the starting point for Muslim education, and reciting it was both an art form and a high honor. Organized in 114 surahs (chapters), the Quran was revealed to Muhammad over a period of some twenty-two years. Often the revelations came in response to particular problems that the young Islamic community and the Prophet were facing. The selections that follow convey something of the Quran's understanding of God, of humankind, of the social life prescribed for believers, of relations with non-Muslims, and much more.

Questions to consider as you examine the source:

■ How does the Quran's understanding of Allah resemble Jewish and Christian ideas about God, and how does it differ from them?

■ What specific prescriptions for social life do these selections contain? Notice in particular those directed toward the weakest members of society. How would you describe the Quran's view of a good society?

■ The sacred texts of all religious traditions provide ample room for conflicting understandings and interpretations. What debates or controversies might arise from these passages?

The Quran
Seventh Century C.E.

On God/Allah

In the name of God, the infinitely compassionate and infinitely merciful. Praise be to God, Lord of all the worlds; the compassionate, the merciful; Ruler on the Day of Reckoning. You alone do we worship, and You alone do we ask for help. Guide us on the straight path, the path of those who have received your grace, not the path of those who have brought down wrath, nor of those who wander astray. (1:1–7)

In the name of Allah, the beneficent, the merciful. Say: He is Allah, the One. He is Allah, the eternal, who was never born nor ever gave birth. The One beyond compare. (112:1–4)

Wherever you turn, there is the face of God. (2:115)

Now verily, it is We who have created man, and We know what his innermost self whispers within him: for We are closer to him than his neck-vein. (50:16)

We will show them Our signs on the farthest horizons, and within their own selves, until it becomes manifest to them that this is the Truth. (41:53)

On Jesus

Behold! the angels said, "Oh Mary! God gives you glad tidings of a Word from Him. His name will be Christ Jesus, the son of Mary, held in honour in this world and the Hereafter, and in (the company of) those nearest to God. He shall speak to the people in childhood and in maturity. He shall be (in the company) of the righteous. . . . And God will teach him the Book and Wisdom, the Law and the Gospel." (3:45–48)

On Society

And thus have We willed you to be a community of the middle way, so that [with your lives] you might bear witness to the truth before all mankind. . . . (2:143)

Behold, those who sinfully devour the possessions of orphans but fill their bellies with fire: for [in the life to come] they will have to endure a blazing flame! (4:10)

You shall do good unto your parents and kinsfolk, and the orphans, and the poor; and you shall speak unto all people in a kindly way; and you shall be constant in prayer; and you shall spend in charity. (2:83)

And if any of those whom you rightfully possess [slaves] desire [to obtain] a deed of freedom, write it out for them if you are aware of any good in them: and give them [their] share of the wealth of God which He has given you. And do not, in order to gain some of the fleeting pleasures of this worldly life, coerce your [slave] maidens into whoredom if they happen to be desirous of marriage. . . . (24:33)

On Men and Women

Verily, for all men and women who have surrendered themselves unto God . . . , and all men and women who give in charity, and all self-denying men and self-denying women, and all men and women who are mindful of their chastity, and all men and women who remember God unceasingly: for [all of] them has God readied forgiveness of sins and a mighty reward. (33:35)

Men are the protectors and maintainers of women, because God has given the one more (strength) than the other, and because they support them from their means. Therefore the righteous women are devoutly obedient, and guard in (the husband's) absence what God would have them guard. As to those women on whose part ye fear disloyalty and ill-conduct, admonish them (first), (Next), refuse to share their beds, (And last) beat them (lightly); but if they return to obedience, seek not against them Means (of annoyance): For God is Most High, great (above you all). (4:34)

O you who believe. You are forbidden to inherit women against their will. Nor should you treat them with harshness. . . . On the contrary, live with them on a footing of kindness and equity. (4:19)

On War and Jihad

There shall be no coercion in matters of faith. (2:256)

And fight in God's cause against those who wage war against you, but do not commit aggression, for, verily, God does not love aggressors. And slay them wherever you may come upon them, and drive them away from wherever they drove you away, for oppression is even worse than killing. And fight not against them near the Inviolable House of Worship unless they fight against you there first, but if they fight against you, slay them: such shall be the recompense of those who deny the truth. (2:190–92)

Now when you meet [in war] those who are bent on denying the truth, smite their necks until you overcome them fully, and then tighten their bonds; but thereafter [set them free,] either by an act of grace or against ransom, so that the burden of war may be lifted. . . . And as for those who are slain in God's cause, never will He let their deeds go to waste. (47:4)

On Tolerance

And tell My servants that they should speak in the most kindly manner [unto those who do not share their beliefs]: verily, Satan is always ready to stir up discord between men. . . . (17:53)

Unto every community have We appointed [different] ways of worship, which they ought to observe. (22:67)

Unto every one of you have We appointed a [different] law and way of life. And if God had so willed, He could surely have made you all one single community: but [He willed it otherwise] in order to test you. . . . Vie, then, with one another in doing good works! (5:48)

All believers are but brethren. Hence, [whenever they are at odds,] make peace between your two brethren, and remain conscious of God, so that you might be graced with His mercy. (49:10)

Make no distinction between any of God's messengers; for they all say, "We have heard and we pay heed." Grant us your forgiveness, O our Sustainer, for it is with You that all journeys end. (2:285)

Source: Muhammad Asad, *The Message of the Qur'an* (Bristol: Book Foundation, 2003). Reprinted by permission of Kabir Edmund Helminski.

Source 9.2
The Voice of the Prophet Muhammad

As an expression of Islam, the sayings and deeds of Muhammad, known as the hadiths, are second in importance only to the Quran. In various collections of hadiths, Muslims hear the voice and witness the actions of their prophet. While they do not have the authority of divine revelation, these statements have served to guide and inspire Muslims to this day.

In the several centuries following his death, an enormous number of stories about Muhammad circulated within the Islamic community. Scholars gradually developed methods of authentication designed to discover which of these stories most reliably represented the Prophet's words and actions. Considerable controversy accompanied this process, and no single collection of hadiths has ever achieved universal acceptance. One of the earliest and most highly respected of these collections was the work of the Persian scholar al-Bukhari (810–870). Traveling extensively throughout the Islamic world, al-Bukhari is said to have collected some 600,000 stories, memorized 200,000 of them, and finally authenticated and published 7,275. The selections that follow suggest something of the range and variety of the hadiths, particularly as they relate to social life.

Questions to consider as you examine the source:

■ What portrait of Muhammad emerges from this record of his sayings and actions?

■ How do these hadiths reflect or build on the teaching of the Quran in Source 9.1?

■ What religious and social values do these hadiths highlight?

The Hadiths
Eighth and Ninth Centuries

If a slave serves honestly his [earthly] master and worships earnestly his [heavenly] Lord, he will have a double recompense.

He who shows concern for the widows and the unfortunate [ranks as high] as one who goes on Jihad in the way of Allah, or one who fasts by day and who rises at night [for prayer].

In this world be as a stranger, or as one who is just passing along the road.

To look at a woman is forbidden, even if it is a look without desire, so how much the more is touching her.

Said he — upon whom be Allah's blessing and peace — "Avoid seven pernicious things." [His Companions] said: "And what are they, O Apostle of Allah?" He answered: "Associating anything with Allah, sorcery, depriving anyone of life where Allah has forbidden that save for just cause, taking usury, devouring the property of orphans, turning the back on the day of battle, and slandering chaste believing women even though they may be acting carelessly."

To be stationed on the frontier for one day during Holy War is better than (to possess) this world and all that is on it. A place in Paradise the size of one of your whip-lashes is better than this world and all that is on it. . . .

If a man sees something in [the conduct of] his ruler which he dislikes let him put up with it patiently, for there is no one who separates himself even a span from the community and dies [in that separation], but dies a pagan death. . . .

Said the Prophet . . . : "I had a look into Paradise and I saw that the poor made up most of its inhabitants, and I had a look into Hell and saw that most of its inhabitants were women. . . ."

Treat women-folk kindly, for woman was created of a rib.

Said the Apostle of Allah . . . : "O band of youths, let him among you who is able to make a home get married, and let him who is not able

betake himself to fasting for he will find in that a quencher [of his passions]."

The worst of foods is that of a feast to which the rich have been invited and the poor overlooked. . . .

Said the Apostle of Allah . . . : "Do not wear silks and satins, and do not drink from gold and silver vessels nor eat from dishes made thereof, for these things are theirs in this world but ours in the world to come." . . .

Said the Prophet . . . : "He who drinks wine in this world and repents not of it will be forbidden it in the world to come." . . .

Al-Aqra said: "I have ten sons but never have I kissed any one of them." The Apostle of Allah . . . looked at him, and then said: "He who does not show tenderness will not have tenderness shown him."

Source: Arthur Jeffery, ed. and trans., *A Reader on Islam* (The Hague: Mouton, 1962), 81–86. Used by permission of Walter de Gruyter GmbH & Co.

Source 9.3
The Voice of the Law

While Christian scholarship emphasized theology and correct belief, learned Muslims gave more attention to law and correct behavior. That law was known as the sharia, an Arabic term that referred to a path toward water, which is the source of life. To many Muslims, that was the role of law — to construct the good society within which an authentic religious life could find expression.

The sharia emerged as the early Islamic community confronted the practical problems of an expanding empire with a very diverse population. But no single legal framework developed. Rather, four major schools of Islamic law crystallized, agreeing on fundamentals but differing in emphasis. How much weight should be given to the hadiths, and which of them were most reliably authentic? What scope should reason and judgment have in applying religious principles to particular circumstances? Despite disagreement on such questions, each of the four approaches to legal interpretation sought to be all-embracing, providing highly detailed guidance on ritual performance, personal behavior, marriage and family matters, crime and punishment, economic transactions, and political action. The selections that follow, drawn from various legal traditions, illustrate this comprehensive nature of Islamic law and its centrality in an evolving Islamic civilization.

Questions to consider as you examine the source:

■ In what ways do these selections draw on and apply the teachings of the Quran and the hadiths?

■ Why do you think the role of law was so central, so highly detailed, and so comprehensive in Islamic civilization?

■ What do this document and Source 9.2 suggest about the problems that the early Islamic community confronted?

The Sharia
Ninth Century

On Prayer

The five prayers are obligatory for every Muslim who has reached the age of puberty and has the use of reason, except for women who are menstruating or recovering from childbirth.

If Muslims deny the necessity of prayer through ignorance, one must instruct them; if they deny it willfully, they have apostatized. . . .

On Zakat [alms for the poor]

The obligation pertains only to a free Muslim who has complete ownership of the property on which it is due. . . . Zakat is due only on animals, agricultural products, precious metals, objects intended for sale, the products of mines, and treasure troves.

Whoever has the obligation to pay zakat and is able must pay it; if not, they commit a fault for which they must answer. If anyone refuses to pay it and denies its obligatory character, they have committed apostasy and may be put to death. If they refuse it from avarice, they shall have the amount taken from them and be given a sentence at the judge's discretion.

On Marriage

[Marriage] is contracted by means of declaration and consent. When both parties are Muslims, it must be contracted in the presence of two male or one male and two female Muslim witnesses who are free, sane, and adult. . . .

It is not lawful for a man to marry two women who are sisters or to cohabit with two sisters who are his slaves. . . .

A man may not marry his slave-girl unless he sets her free first, and a woman may not marry her slave, since marriage has as its object that the children belong equally to both parents, and ownership and slavery are not equal states.

Similarly, marriage with an idolatress is forbidden, until she accepts Islam or a religion of the Book.

It is not lawful for a man already married to a free woman to marry a slave. . . . However, a man may lawfully marry a free woman after a slave.

A free man may marry four women, free or slave, but no more. It is unlawful for a slave to marry more than two women. . . .

On Government

There are ten things a Caliph [successor to Muhammad as political leader of the Islamic community] must do in public affairs:

1. Maintain religion according to its established principles.

2. Apply legal judgments for litigants so that equity reigns without aiding the oppressor or weakening the oppressed.

3. Protect the flock . . . so that people may gain their living and move from place to place securely.

4. Apply the hudud, or punishments of the Law, so as to secure God's prohibitions from violation.

5. Fortify the marches so that the enemy will not appear due to neglect, shedding the blood of any Muslim or protected person.

6. Wage jihad against those who reject Islam so that they become either Muslims or protected people.

7. Collect the zakat and taxes on conquered territory . . . without fear or oppression.

8. Administer treasury expenditures.

9. Delegate loyal and trustworthy people.

10. Directly oversee matters and not delegate his authority seeking to occupy himself with either pleasure or devotion. . . .

It is necessary therefore to cause the masses to act in accord with divine laws in all the affairs, both in this world and in the world to come. The authority to do so was possessed by the prophets and after them by their successors.

On Men and Women

It is not permitted to men or women to eat or drink or keep unguents [ointments] in vessels of gold or silver. . . .

It is not permitted for a man to wear silk, but it is permitted for a woman. . . .

It is not permitted for a man to wear gold or silver, except for silver on a ring, or on a weapon.

It is not permitted for a man to look at a strange woman [a woman outside one's immediate family]. . . . A woman frequently needs to bare her hands and face in transactions with men. Abu Hanifa said it was also permitted to look at her feet and Abu Yusuf said it was permitted to look at her forearms as well. . . . However, if a man is not secure from feeling lust, he should not look needlessly even at the face or hands, to avoid sin. He is not allowed to touch her face or hands even if he is free from lust, whether he be young or old.

On the Economy

It is disliked to corner the market in food for humans or animals if it occurs in a town where this may prove harmful to the people. It is disliked to sell weapons in a time of trouble.

There is no harm in selling fruit juice to someone who will make wine of it, since the transgression is not in the juice but in the wine after it has been changed. . . .

Earning a living by changing money is a great danger to the religion of the one who practices it. . . . It is the duty of the muhtasib [inspector of the markets] to search out the money changers' places of business and spy on them, and if he finds one of them practicing usury or doing something illegal . . . he must punish that person. . . .

Owners of ships and boats must be prevented from loading their vessels above the usual load, for fear of sinking. . . . If they carry women on the same boat with men, there must be a partition between them.

Sellers of [pottery] are not to overlay any that are pierced or cracked with gypsum . . . and then sell them as sound.

Source: John Alden Williams. "The Voice of the Law: The Sharia." Excerpt from *The Word of Islam*, edited by John Alden Williams. Copyright © 1994. By permission of the University of Texas Press.

Source 9.4
The Voice of the Sufis

Alongside the law ran a very different current of Islamic thinking and expression known as Sufism. The Sufis, sometimes called the "friends of God," were the mystics of Islam, those for whom the direct, personal, and intoxicating experience of Divine Presence was of far greater importance than the laws, regulations, and judgments of the sharia. Sufism was a current of many streams within the Islamic world. Some were given to ecstatic states of consciousness, while others were more sober. Some were affiliated directly with established political authorities, while others were critical of those authorities or sought to remain uninvolved with political life. Organized in hundreds of separate orders, or "brotherhoods," each with its own sheiks or teachers, its own distinctive lineage and practices, its own lodges, the Sufis constituted one of the transregional networks that linked the far-flung domains of the Islamic world. Often they were the missionaries of Islam, introducing the faith to Anatolia, India, Central Asia, and other regions.

Among the most prominent exemplars of Sufi sensibility was Rumi (1207–1273), born in what is now Afghanistan and raised in a Persian cultural tradition. Rumi's family later migrated to Anatolia, and Rumi lived most of his adult life in the city of Konya, where he is buried. There he wrote extensively, including a six-volume work of rhymed couplets known as the *Mathnawi*. Following Rumi's death, his son established the Mevlevi Sufi order, based on Rumi's teachings and known in the West as the "whirling dervishes," on account of the turning dances that became a part of their practice.

Rumi's poetry has remained a sublime expression of the mystical dimension of Islamic spiritual seeking and has provided inspiration and direction for millions, both within and beyond the Islamic world. In the early twenty-first century, Rumi was the best-selling poet in the United States. The selections that follow provide a brief sample of the Sufi approach to religious life.

Questions to consider as you examine the source:

- How would you define the religious sensibility of Rumi's poetry?

- How does Rumi's approach to Islam differ from the approach reflected in the sharia?

- What criticisms might the orthodox legal scholars (ulama) have made regarding the Sufi understanding of Islam?

Source 9.4A
Inscription in Rumi's Tomb
Thirteenth Century

Come, come, whoever you are,
Wanderer, worshipper, lover of leaving.
It doesn't matter.
Ours is not a caravan of despair.

Come, even if you have broken your vow a thousand times,
Come, yet again, come, come.

Source: A frequently quoted inscription hanging inside the tomb of Rumi and generally, though not universally, attributed to him; translator unknown.

Source 9.4B
RUMI

Poem
Thirteenth Century

I searched for God among the Christians and on the
*   Cross and therein I found Him not.*
I went into the ancient temples of idolatry; no trace of
*   Him was there.*
I entered the mountain cave of Hira and then went as
*   far as Qandhar but God I found not. . . .*
Then I directed my search to the Kaaba, the resort of
*   old and young; God was not there even.*

Turning to philosophy I inquired about him from ibn
*   Sina but found Him not within his range. . . .*
Finally, I looked into my own heart and there I saw
*   Him; He was nowhere else.*

Source: M. M. Sharif, *A History of Muslim Philosophy*, vol. 2, copyright © 1966 (Wiesbaden: Harrassowitz, 1966), 2:838. Used by permission of Otto Harrassowitz, GmbH & Co. KG.

Source 9.4C
RUMI

Mathnawi
Thirteenth Century

Whether one moves slowly or with speed
the one who is a seeker will be a finder.
Always seek with your whole self,
for the search is an excellent guide on the way.
Though you are lame and limping,
though your figure is bent and clumsy,
always creep towards the One. Make that One your
*   quest.*
By speech and by silence and by fragrance,
catch the scent of the king everywhere.

Listen, open a window to God
and begin to delight yourself
by gazing upon Him through the opening.
The business of love is to make that window in the
*   heart. . . .*
Gaze incessantly on the face of the Beloved!
Listen, this is in your power, my friend.

Source: From *Jewels of Remembrance*, by Rumi, selected and translated by Camille and Kabir Helminski, © 1996 by Camille and Kabir Helminski. Reprinted by arrangement with The Permissions Company, Inc., on behalf of Shambhala Publications Inc., Boston, MA, www.shambhala.com.

Source 9.5
Islamic Practice in West Africa

The preceding four sources reflect the diverse voices of Islam as they were expressed in sacred text and teachings. The next two focus on diversity in practice. Source 9.5 derives from the experience of the widely travelled Ibn Battuta (1304–1368), a Moroccan Muslim, who journeyed as a pilgrim, a Sufi religious seeker, and a legal scholar and frequently traveled in the company of Muslim merchants. Among the many places he visited was West Africa, where the faith had been introduced by North African Muslim traders and had found a growing acceptance, particularly in the urban centers, merchant communities, and ruling classes of West African kingdoms such as Mali. As a highly educated Arab visitor from the established heartland of Islam, Ibn Battuta was often critical of the quality of Islamic observance in the frontier regions of the faith such as West Africa. His account of life in fourteenth-century Mali illustrates the considerable variation that accompanied the practice of Islam across the vast expanse of the Islamic world.

Questions to consider as you examine the source:

■ How would you describe Ibn Battuta's impression of Mali? What surprised or shocked him? What did he appreciate?

■ What does Ibn Battuta's description of his visit to Mali reveal about his own attitudes and his image of himself?

■ What might historians learn from this document about the nature and extent of Islam's penetration in this West African empire? What elements of older and continuing West African cultural traditions are evident in the document? In what ways did Mali interact with the wider world of Islam?

IBN BATTUTA
Travels in Asia and Africa
1354

Thus we reached the town of Iwalatan after a journey . . . [across the Sahara Desert] of two months to a day. Iwalatan is the northernmost province of the blacks. . . . The garments of its inhabitants . . . are of fine Egyptian fabrics.

Their women are of surpassing beauty, and are shown more respect than the men. The state of affairs amongst these people is indeed extraordinary. Their men show no signs of jealousy whatever; no one claims descent from his father, but on the contrary from his mother's brother. A person's heirs are his sister's sons, not his own sons. This is a thing which I have seen nowhere in the world except among the Indians of Malabar. But those are heathens; these people are Muslims, punctilious in observing the hours of prayer, studying books of law, and memorizing the Koran [Quran]. Yet their women show no bashfulness before men and do not veil themselves, though they are assiduous in attending the prayers.

The women there have "friends" and "companions" amongst the men outside their own families, and the men in the same way have "companions" amongst the women of other families. A man may go into his house and find his wife entertaining her "companion," but he takes no objection to it. One day at Iwalatan I went into the qadi's [an Islamic judge] house, after asking his permission to enter, and found with him a young woman of remarkable beauty. When I saw her I was shocked and turned to go out, but she laughed at me, instead of being overcome by shame, and the qadi said to me "Why are you going out? She is my companion." I was amazed at their conduct, for he was a theologian and a pilgrim [to Mecca] to boot. . . .

Thus I reached the city of Malli, the capital of the king of the blacks. I stopped at the cemetery and went to the quarter occupied by the whites. . . . I met the qadi of Malli, 'Abd ar-Rahman, who came to see me; he is a black, a pilgrim [to Mecca], and a man of fine character. I met also the interpreter Dugha, who is one of the principal men among the blacks. All these persons sent me hospitality gifts of food and treated me with the utmost generosity. . . .

The sultan [ruler] of Malli is Mansa Sulayman. . . . He is a miserly king, not a man from whom one might hope for a rich present. It happened that I spent these two months without seeing him, on account of my illness. Later on he held a banquet . . . to which the commanders, doctors, qadis, and preachers were invited, and I went along with them. Reading-desks were brought in, and the Koran was read through. . . .

When the ceremony was over I went forward and saluted Mansa Sulayman. . . . When I withdrew, the [sultan's] hospitality gift was sent to me. . . . I stood up thinking . . . that it consisted of robes of honor and money, and lo!, it was three cakes of bread, and a piece of beef fried in native oil, and a calabash of sour curds. When I saw this I

burst out laughing, and thought it a most amazing thing that they could be so foolish and make so much of such a paltry matter.

On certain days the sultan holds audiences in the palace yard, where there is a platform under a tree, with three steps. . . . It is carpeted with silk and has cushions placed on it. [Over it] is raised the umbrella, which is a sort of pavilion made of silk, surmounted by a bird in gold, about the size of a falcon. The sultan comes out of a door in a corner of the palace, carrying a bow in his hand and a quiver on his back. On his head he has a golden skullcap, bound with a gold band which has narrow ends shaped like knives, more than a span in length. His usual dress is a velvety red tunic, made of the European fabrics called "mutanfas." The sultan is preceded by his musicians, who carry gold and silver guimbris [a two-stringed guitar], and behind him come three hundred armed slaves. He walks in a leisurely fashion, affecting a very slow movement, and even stops from time to time. On reaching the [platform] he stops and looks round the assembly, then ascends it in the sedate manner of a preacher ascending a mosque-pulpit. As he takes his seat the drums, trumpets, and bugles are sounded. Three slaves go out at a run to summon the sovereign's deputy and the military commanders, who enter and sit down. Two saddled and bridled horses are brought, along with two goats, which they hold to serve as a protection against the evil eye. . . .

The blacks are of all people the most submissive to their king and the most abject in their behavior before him. . . . If he summons any of them while he is holding an audience in his pavilion, the person summoned takes off his clothes and puts on worn garments, removes his turban and dons a dirty skullcap, and enters with his garments and trousers raised knee-high. He goes forward in an attitude of humility and dejection and knocks the ground hard with his elbows, then stands with bowed head and bent back listening to what he says. If anyone addresses the king and receives a reply from him, he uncovers his back and throws dust over his head and back, for all the world like a bather splashing himself with water. . . .

On feast-days . . . , the poets come in. Each of them is inside a figure resembling a thrush, made of feathers, and provided with a wooden head with a red beak, to look like a thrush's head. They stand in front of the sultan in this ridiculous makeup and recite their poems. I was told that their poetry is a kind of sermonizing in which they say to the sultan: "This [platform] which you occupy was that whereon sat this king and that king, and such and such were this one's noble actions and such and such the other's. So do you too do good deeds whose memory will outlive you." . . . I was told that this practice is a very old custom amongst them, prior to the introduction of Islam, and that they have kept it up.

The blacks possess some admirable qualities. They are seldom unjust, and have a greater abhorrence of injustice than any other people. Their sultan shows no mercy to anyone who is guilty of the least act of it. There is complete security in their country. Neither traveler nor inhabitant in it has anything to fear from robbers or men of violence. They do not confiscate the property of any white man who dies in their country, even if it be uncounted wealth. On the contrary, they give it into the charge of some trustworthy person among the whites, until the rightful heir takes possession of it. They are careful to observe the hours of prayer, and assiduous in attending them in congregations, and in bringing up their children to them.

On Fridays, if a man does not go early to the mosque, he cannot find a corner to pray in, on account of the crowd. It is a custom of theirs to send each man his boy [to the mosque] with his prayer-mat; the boy spreads it out for his master in a place befitting him [and remains on it] until he comes to the mosque. . . .

Another of their good qualities is their habit of wearing clean white garments on Fridays. Even if a man has nothing but an old worn shirt, he washes it and cleans it, and wears it to the Friday service. Yet another is their zeal for learning the Koran by heart. . . . I visited the qadi in his house on the day of the festival. His children were chained up, so I said to him, "Will you not let them loose?" He replied, "I shall not do so until they learn the Koran by heart."

Among their bad qualities are the following. The women servants, slave-girls, and young girls go about in front of everyone naked, without a stitch of clothing on them. Women go into the sultan's presence naked and without coverings, and his daughters also go about naked. Then there is their custom of putting dust and ashes on their heads, as a mark of respect, and the grotesque ceremonies we have described when the poets recite their verses. Another reprehensible practice among many of them is the eating of carrion, dogs, and asses.

Source: Ibn Battuta, *Travels in Asia and Africa, 1325–1354*, translated and edited by H. A. R. Gibb (London: Broadway House, 1929), 319–34. Used by permission of the Hakluyt Society.

Source 9.6
Men and Women at Worship

Differences in Islamic practice occurred not only among various regions or cultural settings but also between men and women, even in a single mosque, as illustrated in this sixteenth-century Persian painting. The setting involves the visit of a prominent teacher to a mosque, an event that drew a large and varied congregation. The guest teacher, on the left, sits at the top of a raised platform or pulpit. The rest of the congregation is distributed at various distances from him according to age and gender.

Questions to consider as you examine the source:

- How would you describe the social organization of this event?

- What variations among the men in the main hall of the mosque can you identify? Notice especially their head coverings and beards, or lack of them.

- What does the image suggest about the location of the women in the mosque? What variations among the women can you identify?

Men and Women at Worship

Voices of Islam

1. **Defining differences within Islam:** In what different ways do the various voices of Islam represented in these sources understand and express the common religious tradition of which they are all a part? What grounds for debate or controversy can you identify within or among them?

2. **Defining a good society:** On what elements of a good society might Muslims agree? How might they differ?

3. **Considering gender and Islam:** How do these sources represent the roles of men and women in Islamic society? Pay particular attention to differences in emphasis.

4. **Seeking additional sources:** Notice that all of these sources derive from literate elites, and each of them suggests or prescribes appropriate behavior. What additional documents would you need if you were to assess the impact of these prescriptions on the lives of ordinary people? What specific questions might you want to pose to such documents?

THINKING THROUGH SOURCES

The Crusades as Cultural Encounter

For two centuries (1095–1291), Christian armies from Western Europe periodically invaded the Middle East to recapture for Christendom the Holy Lands associated with the life of Jesus, which then lay under the control of Muslim powers. These efforts became the most widely known expression of the "Crusades," holy wars authorized by the pope to extend or protect the interests of Christianity. From the viewpoint of the Islamic world, they represented naked and brutal aggression. Many Christians, however, saw them as defensive, a response to the earlier Arab Muslim invasion of Christian lands and to the recent threat of Turkic Muslim incursions against the Byzantine Empire. Either way, they were an episode in a much longer encounter of Christian and Islamic civilizations.

Historians have focused much of their study on the origins of the Crusades and on the military conflicts they generated. Initial Crusader victories resulted in the establishment of four small Christian states in the Holy Land, including one in Jerusalem. But by 1291, Muslim forces had recaptured all of them. Here, however, our attention shifts to the cultural side of this epic encounter — how various peoples perceived or understood one another. As a vast set of cultural encounters, the Crusades encompassed more than Christians and Muslims. European and Middle Eastern Jews were likewise caught up in the Crusades, while relationships between Latin Catholic and Greek Orthodox Christians figured prominently in them as well. In assessing the sources that follow, we are less interested in "what really happened" than in the impressions, images, perceptions, and stereotypes that the various participants in the Crusades held of one another.

Source 10.1
A Western Christian Perspective:
Pope Urban II

The Crusades began in 1095 when Pope Urban II issued a stirring call to arms, inviting the knights and warriors of Europe to come to the aid of the Byzantine Empire and Eastern Christians, increasingly threatened by Turkish Muslim forces, and to liberate Jerusalem from Muslim control. Several versions of this famous speech have survived, including one from a French archbishop named Baldric, who included it in a history of the First Crusade, written in 1107.

Questions to consider as you examine the source:

- How does the pope justify his call for military action against Muslims?

- What views of the Islamic world are reflected in this speech? What did Muslim occupation of formerly Christian sites mean to the pope?

- Does the fact that this account was written after the Christian victory in the First Crusade affect its usefulness to historians?

POPE URBAN II

Speech at Clermont

1095

We have heard . . . with great hurt and dire sufferings how our Christian brothers . . . are scourged, oppressed, and injured in Jerusalem, in Antioch, and the other cities of the East. Your own blood brothers . . . are either subjected in their inherited homes to other masters, or are driven from them, or they come as beggars among us; or, which is far worse, they are flogged and exiled as slaves for sale in their own land. Christian blood . . . and Christian flesh, akin to the flesh of Christ, has been subjected to unspeakable degradation and servitude. . . . The churches in which divine mysteries were celebrated in olden times are now . . . used as stables for the animals of these people! Holy men do not possess those cities; nay, base and bastard Turks hold sway over our brothers. . . . [T]he Gentiles [Muslims] have established their superstitions, and the Christian religion, which they ought rather to cherish, they have basely shut out from the hall [church] dedicated to God! . . . The priesthood of God has been ground down into the dust. The sanctuary of God (unspeakable shame) is everywhere profaned. Whatever Christians still remain in hiding there are sought out with unheard of tortures.

[H]oly Jerusalem . . . this very city, in which Christ Himself suffered for us, because our sins demanded it, has been reduced to the pollution of paganism and . . . withdrawn from the service of God. Such is the heap of reproach upon us who have so much deserved it! . . . The Turks violently took from [the tomb of Christ] the offerings which you brought there for alms in such vast amounts, and, in addition, they scoffed much and often at your religion. . . . Woe unto us, brethren! We who have already become a reproach to our neighbors . . . let us at least with tears condone and have compassion upon our brothers! . . . This land we have deservedly called holy in which there is not even a footstep that the body or spirit of the Saviour did not render glorious and blessed, which embraced the holy presence of the mother of God, and the meetings of the apostles, and drank up the blood of the martyrs shed there. . . .

What are we saying? Listen and learn! You, girt about with the badge of knighthood, are arrogant with great pride; you rage against your brothers and cut each other in pieces. You, the oppressors of children, plunderers of widows; you, guilty of homicide, of sacrilege, robbers of another's rights; . . . you sense battles from afar and rush to them eagerly. Verily, this is the worst way, for it is utterly removed from God! if, forsooth, you wish to be mindful of your souls, either lay down the girdle of such knighthood, or advance boldly, as knights of Christ, and rush as quickly as you can to the defense of the Eastern Church. . . .

We say this, brethren, that you may restrain your murderous hands from the destruction of your brothers, and in behalf of your relatives in the faith oppose yourselves to the Gentiles. . . . [M]ay you deem it a beautiful thing to die for Christ in that city in which He died for us. You should shudder, brethren, at raising a violent hand against Christians; it is less wicked to brandish your sword against Saracens [Muslims]. It is the only warfare that is righteous, for it is charity to risk your life for your brothers. . . . The possessions of the enemy, too, will be yours, since you will make spoil of their treasures and return victorious to your own; or empurpled with your own blood, you will have gained everlasting glory.

Gird yourselves, everyone of you, I say, and be valiant sons; for it is better for you to die in battle than to behold the sorrows of your race and of your holy places. Let neither property nor the alluring charms of your wives entice you from going; nor let the trials that are to be borne so deter you that you remain here.

[*According to Baldric, the pope turned to the bishops and said:*] You, brothers and fellow bishops; you, fellow priests and sharers with us in Christ, make this same announcement through the churches committed to you, and with your whole soul vigorously preach the journey to Jerusalem. When they have confessed the disgrace of their sins, do you, secure in Christ, grant them speedy pardon. Moreover, you who are to go shall have us praying for you.

Source: August C. Krey, *The First Crusade: The Accounts of Eye-Witnesses and Participants* (Princeton, NJ: Princeton University Press, 1921), 33–36.

Source 10.2
Jewish Experience of the Crusades

European anti-Semitism had a long history and many expressions. The old idea that the Jews were responsible for the death of Jesus provided a religious basis for hatred of the Jews. Their economic marginalization into occupations deemed impure although necessary, such as tax collection and moneylending, engendered hostility. These conditions, in combination with distinctive Jewish religious practices, gave rise to any number of stereotypes and negative images: Jews had magical powers derived from a pact with the devil; Jews murdered Christian children and drank their blood; Jews deliberately desecrated the host or communion wafers used in Catholic worship. Depending on time and place, Jews could be forbidden to own land or practice certain trades, forced to live in restricted areas, subjected to special taxes, and required to dress in distinctive ways. All of this marked Jews as "other," distinctly different from their Christian neighbors.

The Crusades provided an opportunity for this European anti-Semitism to be expressed in action. On a number of occasions some Crusaders on their way to the Middle East took time to wreak havoc on Jewish communities in Europe, although such actions were widely condemned by political and religious authorities. Source 10.2 provides a description of these horrendous attacks in 1096, written by a twelfth-century Christian historian named Albert of Aix-la-Chapelle based on interviews with returning Crusaders. He was not a participant in the Crusades or an eyewitness to the events he describes.

Questions to consider as you examine the source:

- What is Albert's posture toward these attacks?

- How did Jews attempt to protect themselves from these attacks?

- To what extent did Albert distinguish among various kinds of Christians?

An Account of Attacks on Jews during the First Crusade
Early to Mid-Twelfth Century

At the beginning of summer in the same year [1096] in which Peter and Gottschalk [leaders of the First Crusade], after collecting an army, had set out, there assembled in like fashion a large and innumerable host of Christians from diverse kingdoms and lands; namely, from the realms of France, England, Flanders, and Lorraine. . . . I know not whether by a judgment of the Lord, or by some error of mind, they rose in a spirit of cruelty against the Jewish people scattered throughout these cities and slaughtered them without mercy, especially in the Kingdom of Lorraine, asserting it to be the beginning of their expedition and their duty against the enemies of the Christian faith. This slaughter of Jews was done first by citizens of Cologne. These suddenly fell upon a small band of Jews and severely wounded and killed many; they destroyed the houses and synagogues of the Jews and divided among themselves a very large amount of money. When the Jews saw this cruelty, about two hundred in the silence of the night began flight by boat to Neuss. The pilgrims and crusaders discovered them, and after taking away all their possessions, inflicted on them similar slaughter, leaving not even one alive.

Not long after this, they started upon their journey, as they had vowed, and arrived in a great multitude at the city of Mainz. There Count Emico, a nobleman, a very mighty man in this region, was awaiting, with a large band of Teutons, the arrival of the pilgrims who were coming thither from diverse lands by the King's highway.

The Jews of this city, knowing of the slaughter of their brethren, and that they themselves could not escape the hands of so many, fled in hope of safety to Bishop Rothard. They put an infinite treasure in his guard and trust, having much faith in his protection, because he was Bishop of the city. Then that excellent Bishop of the city cautiously set aside the incredible amount of money received from them. He placed the Jews in the very spacious hall of his own house, away from the sight of Count Emico and his followers, that they might remain safe and sound in a very secure and strong place.

But Emico and the rest of his band held a council and, after sunrise, attacked the Jews in the hall with arrows and lances. Breaking the bolts and doors, they killed the Jews, about seven hundred in number, who in vain resisted the force and attack of so many thousands. They killed the women, also, and with their swords pierced tender children of whatever age and sex. The Jews, seeing that their Christian enemies were attacking them and their children, and that they were sparing no age, likewise fell upon one another, brother, children, wives, and sisters, and thus they perished at each other's hands. Horrible to say, mothers cut the throats of nursing children with knives and stabbed others, preferring them to perish thus by their own hands rather than to be killed by the weapons of the uncircumcised.

From this cruel slaughter of the Jews a few escaped; and a few because of fear, rather than because of love of the Christian faith, were baptized. With very great spoils taken from these people, Count Emico, Clarebold, Thomas, and all that intolerable company of men and women then continued on their way to Jerusalem. . . .

So the hand of the Lord is believed to have been against the pilgrims who had sinned by excessive impurity and fornication, and who had slaughtered the exiled Jews through greed of money, rather than for the sake of God's justice, although the Jews were opposed to Christ. The Lord is a just judge and orders no one unwillingly, or under compulsion, to come under the yoke of the Catholic faith.

Source: August. C. Krey, *The First Crusade: The Accounts of Eye-Witnesses and Participants* (Princeton, NJ: Princeton University Press, 1921), 54–56.

Source 10.3
Muslim Perspectives on the Crusades

Well before the Crusades, Muslim impressions of the Christians, who they called Franks, were stereotypical and negative. In a word, they were uncivilized barbarians — personally dirty, sexually promiscuous, and allowing their women altogether too much independence. According to one Arab writer of the twelfth century, Europeans were "animals, possessing the virtues of courage and fighting, nothing else." The Crusades hardened and supplemented such perceptions.

Beyond the trauma of invasion and military defeat during the First Crusade, the very presence of the Christians defiled the sacred spaces of Islam, cutting Muslims off from God. Particularly offensive was the placing of a Christian cross atop the beloved Dome of the Rock. Widely associated with filth, disease, and contamination, the Crusaders were also seen as a threat to the sanctity of Muslim women. Moreover, as Muslims became aware of the fundamentally religious impulses that motivated the Crusaders, their perception of the differences between Islam and Christianity sharpened. The Christian faith seemed to many Muslims absurd and immoral. If Jesus was God, why could he not prevent his own humiliating death? And what kind of god would be born from a woman's private parts? Both the divinity of Jesus and the doctrine of the Trinity flew in the face of Islam's firm monotheism.[1]

One Muslim perspective on the Crusades derives from the writing of the Arab historian Ibn al-Athir. Known as *The Complete History*, his book was composed around 1231 and contained an extensive account of the Crusades. In the excerpts provided here, he begins with a description of the Europeans' bloody conquest of Jerusalem in 1099, followed by a portrayal of the Muslim retaking of the Holy City in 1187. The latter event had occurred under the leadership of Saladin, a heroic figure to Muslims, for he had unified the fragmented Muslim Middle East and had begun to push the Crusaders out. A final brief selection by the Persian historian Imad ad-Din recounts the aftermath of Saladin's victory.

Questions to consider as you examine the source:

■ What differences does al-Athir notice between these two events?

■ What general impression of the Franks comes across in these selections? Is it a wholly negative image or can you identify some nuance in these descriptions of them?

■ How does al-Athir's portrayal of Saladin contribute, by contrast, to his description of the Franks?

IBN AL-ATHIR
The Complete History
ca. 1231

Jerusalem was taken . . . on the morning of Friday 22 sha'ban 492 / 15 July 1099. The population was put to the sword by the Franks, who pillaged the area for a week. A band of Muslims barricaded themselves into the Tower of David and fought on for several days. They were granted their lives in return for surrendering. The Franks honored their word, and the group left by night. . . . In the Masjid al-Aqsa [a major mosque] the Franks slaughtered more than 70,000 people, among them a large number of Imams [leaders of worship in mosques] and Muslim scholars, devout and ascetic men who had left their homelands to live lives of pious seclusion in the Holy Place. The Franks stripped the Dome of the Rock of more than forty silver candelabra, . . . and a great silver lamp as well as a hundred and fifty smaller silver candelabra and more than twenty gold ones, and a great deal more booty.

[Muslim] refugees from Syria reached Baghdad in Ramadan [the month of fasting]. . . . They told the Caliph's ministers a story that wrung their hearts and brought tears to their eyes. On Friday they went to the Cathedral Mosque and begged for help, weeping so that their hearers wept with them as they described the sufferings of the Muslims in that Holy City: the men killed, the women and children taken prisoner, the homes pillaged. Because of the terrible hardships they had suffered, they were allowed to break the fast. It

was the discord between the Muslim princes that enabled the Franks to overrun the country.

[*Now al-Athir's account turns to the Muslim retaking of Jerusalem in 1187.*]

When the Franks saw how violently the Muslims were attacking, . . . meeting no resistance, they grew desperate, and their leaders assembled to take counsel. They decided to ask for safe conduct out of the city and to hand Jerusalem over to Saladin. They sent a deputation of their lords and nobles to ask for terms, but when they spoke of it to Saladin he refused to grant their request. "We shall deal with you," he said, "Just as you dealt with the population of Jerusalem when you took it in 492/1099, with murder and enslavement and other such savageries!" The messengers returned empty handed. Then Balian ibn Barzan [an important French noble in the Crusader Kingdom of Jerusalem] asked for safe-conduct for himself so that he might appear before Saladin to discuss developments. Consent was given, and he presented himself and once again began asking for a general amnesty in return for surrender. The sultan still refused his requests and entreaties to show mercy.

Finally, despairing of this approach, Balian said: "Know, O Sultan, that there are very many of us in this city, God alone knows how many. At the moment we are fighting half-heartedly in the hope of saving our lives, hoping to be spared by you as you have spared others; this is because of our horror of death and our love of life. But if we see that death is inevitable, then by God we shall kill our children and our wives, burn our possessions, so as not to leave you with a dinar or a drachma or a single man or woman to enslave. When this is done, we shall pull down the Sanctuary of the Rock and the Masjid al-Aqsa and the other sacred places, slaughtering the Muslim prisoners we hold — 5,000 of them — and killing every horse and animal we possess. Then we shall come out to fight you like men fighting for their lives, when each man, before he falls dead, kills his equals; we shall die with honour, or win a noble victory!"

Then Saladin took counsel with his advisers, all of whom were in favour of his granting the assurances requested by the Franks, without forcing them to take extreme measures whose outcome could not be foreseen. "Let us consider them as being already our prisoners," they said, "and allow them to ransom themselves on terms agreed between us." The Sultan agreed to give the Franks assurances of safety on the understanding that each man, rich and poor alike, should pay ten dinar, children of both sexes two dinar and women five dinar. All who paid this sum within forty days should go free, and those who had not paid at the end of the time should be enslaved. Balian ibn Barzan offered 30,000 dinar as ransom for the poor, which was accepted, and the city surrendered on Friday 27 rajab / 2 October 1187, a memorable day on which the Muslim flags were hoisted over the walls of Jerusalem. . . .

The Grand Patriarch of the Franks left the city with the treasures from the Dome of the Rock, the Masjid al-Agsa, the Church of the Resurrection and others, God alone knows the amount of treasure; he also took an equal quantity of money. Saladin made no difficulties, and when he was advised to sequestrate [seize] the whole lot for Islam, replied that he would not go back on his word. He took only the ten dinar from him, and let him go, heavily escorted, to Tyre.

At the top of the cupola of the Dome of the Rock there was a great gilded cross. When the Muslims entered the city on the Friday, some of them climbed to the top of the cupola to take down the cross. When they reached the top a great cry went up from the city and from outside the walls, the Muslims crying the *Allah akbar* in their joy, the Franks groaning in consternation and grief. So loud and piercing was the cry that the earth shook.

[*Another Muslim historian, Imad ad-Din, writing in the late twelfth century, described the aftermath of Saladin's conquest of Jerusalem.*]

When Saladin accepted the surrender of Jerusalem, he ordered the *mihrab* [a niche in a mosque which points toward Mecca] to be uncovered. . . . Structures between the columns [were] demolished. The spaces created were carpeted with deep carpets instead of matting. . . . [R]eadings of the revealed text [Quran] [were] given, and thus truth triumphed and error was cancelled out. The *Quran* was raised to the throne and the Testaments [Bible] cast down. Prayer mats were laid out and the religious ceremonies performed in their purity. . . . [T]he muezzins [those who made the call to prayer] were there and not the priests; corruption and shame ceased, and men's breaths became quiet and calm again.

Source: *Arab Historians of the Crusades*, edited and translated by Francesco Gabrieli, © 1996 by Routledge and Kegan Paul Ltd. Published by the University of California Press. Used by permission of the University of California Press and by permission of Taylor & Francis Books UK.

Source 11.5
Religious Responses in the Christian World

The horrific experience of the Black Death also caused some people in the Christian world to question fundamental teachings about the mercy and power of God or the usefulness of religious rituals. For some, the plague prompted an orgy of hedonism, perhaps to affirm life in the face of endless death or simply to live to the full in what time remained to them. Most European Christians, however, relied on familiar practices: seeking the aid of parish priests, invoking the intercession of the Virgin Mary, participating in religious processions and pilgrimages, attending mass regularly, increasing attention to private devotion. From church leaders, the faithful heard a message of the plague as God's punishment for sins. Accompanying such ideas were religiously based attacks on prostitutes, homosexuals, and Jews, people whose allegedly immoral behavior or alien beliefs had invited God's retribution.

The most well-known movement reflecting an understanding of the plague as God's judgment on a sinful world was that of the flagellants, whose name derived from the Latin word *flagella*, meaning "whips." The practice of flagellation, whipping oneself or allowing oneself to be whipped, had a long tradition within the Christian world and elsewhere as well. Flagellation served as a penance for sin and as a means of identifying with Christ, who was himself whipped prior to his crucifixion. It reemerged as a fairly widespread practice, especially in Germany, between 1348 and 1350 in response to the initial outbreak of the plague. Its adherents believed that perhaps the terrible wrath of God could be averted by performing this extraordinary act of atonement or penance. Groups of flagellants like those depicted in Source 11.5A moved from city to city, where they called for repentance, confessed their sins, sang hymns, and participated in ritual dances, which climaxed in whipping themselves with knotted cords sometimes embedded with iron points.

The initial and subsequent outbreaks of the plague in Western Europe generated an understandable preoccupation with death and its apparently indiscriminate occurrence. This concern, or obsession, found expression in the Dance of Death, a ritual intended to prevent the plague or to cure the afflicted, which began in France in 1348. During the performance, people would periodically fall to the ground, allowing others to trample on them. By 1400, such performances took place in a number of parish churches and subsequently in more secular settings. The Dance of Death also received artistic expression in a variety of poems and sketches along with paintings like Source 11.5B.

Questions to consider as you examine the sources:

- Does the procession in Source 11.5A seem spontaneous or organized? Do church authorities appear to have instigated or approved this procession?

- In Source 11.5B, what can you infer about the status of the living figures?

- Notice that the living figures face outward toward the viewer rather than toward the entreating death figures on either side of them. What might this mean?

Source 11.5A
The Flagellants

The Flagellants at Doornik in 1349, copy of a miniature from the Chronicle of Aegidius Li Muisis/*Private Collection/Bridgeman Images*

A contemporary representation of the flagellants in the town of Doornik in the Netherlands in 1349.

Source 11.5B
A Culture of Death

This image reproduces a portion of a Dance of Death painting, originally created by the German artist Berndt Notke in 1463 and subsequently restored and reproduced many times. In the inscriptions at the bottom of the painting, each living character addresses a skeletal figure, who in turn makes a reply. Here is the exchange between the empress (shown in a red dress and elaborate head gear) and Death.

I know, Death means me! I was never terrified so greatly! I thought he was not in his right mind, after all, I am young and also an empress. I thought I had a lot of power; I had not thought of him or that anybody could do something against me. Oh, let me live on, this I implore you!

And then Death replies:

Empress, highly presumptuous, I think, you have forgotten me. Fall in! It is now time. You thought I should let you off? No way! And were you ever so much, you must participate in this play, and you others, everybody — Hold on! Follow me, Mr. Cardinal![4]

Source 11.6
The Black Death and European Jews

Extreme and traumatic events such as the plague cry out for explanation so that people can find some sense of orientation in a bewildering and chaotic environment. One such explanation lay in the scapegoating of minorities or outsiders, constructing conspiracies to account for the inexplicable. In France, "beggars and mendicants of various countries" were accused of poisoning wells, tortured to produce confessions, and then burned to death. More frequently the target of such attacks were Jews, who had long been damned as "Christ killers," prohibited from practicing certain occupations, and stereotyped as greedy moneylenders. Many church authorities, however, had encouraged toleration, hoping that Jews might finally convert to

Christianity. But as the plague took hold, accusations against Jews for poisoning wells mounted, as did attacks upon them, confessions extracted under torture, and executions by burning. Conflicting economic interests played an important role in these events. Rulers and city fathers often wanted to preserve the Jews as a source of tax revenue, while those indebted to Jewish lenders might well benefit from their death. This account by the German chronicler Jacob Von Königshofen (1346–1420) illustrates that horrendous process.

Questions to consider as you examine the source:

- What differences of opinion on dealing with Jews appear in this source?

- What mix of motives lay behind these attacks on Jews?

- How do these attacks on Jews compare with those that occurred during the Crusades? See Source 10.2 in the Thinking through Sources feature for Chapter 10.

JACOB VON KÖNIGSHOFEN

About the Great Plague and the Burning of the Jews
ca. Early Fifteenth Century

In the matter of this plague the Jews throughout the world were reviled and accused in all lands of having caused it through the poison which they are said to have put into the water and the wells. . . . For this reason the Jews were burnt all the way from the Mediterranean into Germany . . . , but not in Avignon, for the pope protected them there.

[I]n Basel the citizens marched to the city hall and compelled the council to take an oath that they would burn the Jews, and that they would allow no Jew to enter the city for the next two hundred years. . . . And there was a great indignation and clamor against the deputies from Strasbourg. So finally the Bishop and the lords and the Imperial Cities agreed to do away with the Jews. On . . . St. Valentine's Day [1349] they burnt the Jews on a wooden platform in their cemetery. There were about two thousand people of them. Those who wanted to baptize themselves were spared.

Many small children were taken out of the fire and baptized against the will of their fathers and mothers. And everything that was owed to the Jews was cancelled, and the Jews had to surrender all pledges and notes that they had taken for debts. The council, however, took the cash that the Jews possessed and divided it among the workingmen proportionately. The money was indeed the thing that killed the Jews. If they had been poor and if the feudal lords had not been in debt to them, they would not have been burnt. After this wealth was divided among the artisans, some gave their share to the Cathedral or to the Church on the advice of their confessors. . . .

In some cities the Jews themselves set fire to their houses and cremated themselves.

Source: Jacob Marcus, *The Jew in the Medieval World: A Sourcebook, 315–1791* (New York: JPS, 1938), 43–48, http://www.fordham .edu/halsall/jewish/1348-jewsblackdeath.asp.

Source 11.7
A Government's Response to the Plague

If individuals and families found themselves required to respond to the Black Death, so too did communities and cities. Various urban authorities issued regulations that they hoped might slow or prevent the spread of the disease. A particularly detailed set of ordinances was issued in the northern Italian city of Pistoia in May of 1348. Interestingly, these ordinances were revised several times over the coming month as the authorities adapted their regulations in an effort to address the growing crisis.

Questions to consider as you examine the source:

■ What assumptions underlay these regulations?

■ What difficulties might these ordinances have created for the living residents of Pistoia?

■ What social distinctions are reflected in these regulations?

Ordinances against the Spread of Plague, Pistoia
1348

No citizen or resident of Pistoia shall dare or presume to go to Pisa or Lucca; and no one shall come to Pistoia from those places; penalty 500 pence.

No one shall dare or presume to bring to Pistoia any old linen or woolen cloths, penalty 200 pence, and the cloth to be burnt in the public piazza of Pistoia by the official who discovered it.

The bodies of the dead shall not be removed from the place of death until they have been enclosed in a wooden box, and the lid of planks nailed down so that no stench can escape: penalty 50 pence to be paid by the heirs of the deceased.

To avoid the foul stench which comes from dead bodies, each grave shall be dug two and a half arms-length deep.

Any person attending a funeral shall not accompany the corpse or its kinsmen further than the door of the church where the burial is to take place, or go back to the house where the deceased lived.

When someone dies, no one shall dare or presume to give or send any gift to the house of the deceased.

To avoid waste and unnecessary expense, no one shall dare or presume to wear new clothes during the mourning period or for the next eight days; penalty 25 pence. This shall not apply to the wife of the deceased, who may if she wishes wear a new garment of any fabric without penalty.

No one shall dare or presume to raise a lament or crying for anyone who has died outside Pistoia, or summon a gathering of people other than the kinsfolk and spouse of the deceased, or have bells rung, or use criers or any other means to invite people throughout the city to such a gathering; penalty 25 pence from each person involved. However it is to be understood that none of this applies to the burial of knights, doctors of law, judges, and doctors of physic, whose bodies can be honoured by their heirs at their burial in any way they please.

So that the living are not made ill by rotten and corrupt food, no butcher or retailer of meat shall dare or presume to hang up meat, or keep and sell meat hung up in their storehouse or over their counter.

To avoid harm to men by stink and corruption, there shall in future be no tanning of skins within the city walls of Pistoia.

At the burial of anyone, no bell is to be rung at all, but people are to be summoned and their prayers invited only by word of mouth.

Source: Rosemary Horrox, ed. and trans., *The Black Death* (Manchester: Manchester University Press, 1994), 195–201. Used by permission of the publisher.

ESSAY QUESTIONS

Living and Dying during the Black Death

1. **Making comparisons:** What similarities and differences can you identify in how people experienced and understood the plague, both between and within particular societies?

2. **Religion and the plague:** How might you assess the role of religion in shaping responses to the plague? In what ways might religion have been helpful? And how might it have exacerbated the suffering associated with the plague?

3. **Reflecting on disasters:** What can we learn about how humans react to natural disasters from studying the Black Death? What do these sources reveal about the extent to which humans are in control of their own lives and their own history? In what ways do larger impersonal forces shape our individual lives and our collective histories?

Notes

1. Manfred Ullman, *Islamic Medicine* (Edinburgh: Edinburgh University Press, 1978), 94–95.

2. Quoted in John Aberth, *The Black Death* (Boston: Bedford/St. Martin's, 2005), 85.

3. Quoted in Aberth, *The Black Death,* 115.

4. "Lübeck's Dance of Death," accessed May 29, 2015, http://www.dodedans.com/Etext2.htm.

THINKING THROUGH SOURCES

Early Encounters; First Impressions

During the fifteenth century on the remote far western end of the Eurasian landmass, the government of Portugal initiated a series of maritime explorations with profound implications for the entire world. Spain and other European powers soon followed suit. Their voyages down the coast of West Africa, around the Cape of Good Hope to India, and across the Atlantic to the Americas set in motion a pattern of European expansion that by 1900 had enveloped most of the peoples of the planet — with incalculable consequences that continue to echo to this day. In that epic process, the peoples of Europe and those of Africa, Asia, and the Americas encountered one another in new ways and often for the first time. Here we examine three of these early encounters and the impressions they generated. The limitations of available sources unfortunately dictate a largely Eurocentric focus, for we know much more about how Europeans experienced these encounters than we do about how the people they met experienced them. Everyone, however, shared an inability to imagine the enormously transforming, and often devastating, outcomes of these early interactions. But here our attention is focused on the initial moments of these historic encounters, pregnant as they were with implications for the future.

Source 12.1
Cadamosto in a West African Chiefdom

At the beginning of the fifteenth century, no one could have predicted that the small and poor kingdom of Portugal, operating at the margins of European life, would become a major international power over the next two centuries. But building on a long seafaring tradition in Mediterranean and North African waters, the Portuguese royal family sponsored a series of maritime voyages that took them down the coast of West Africa and in 1498 all the way to India. A global Portuguese empire began to take shape. It was driven by a familiar mixture of motives — to seek a sea route to the luxury goods of the East; to outflank, defeat, and if possible convert Muslims; to ally with any Christians they could find to continue the crusades; and to provide aristocratic warriors an opportunity for military glory and social promotion. These voyages produced any number of first encounters between Europeans and various African societies as the Portuguese explored the region, constructed trading posts and forts, sought gold and slaves, and made modest efforts at missionary activity.

Among the earliest and the most carefully recorded of these first encounters occurred in 1455, when the Italian trader and explorer Alvise da Cadamosto, sailing for Portugal, encountered Budomel, the ruler of a small chiefdom within the Wolof-speaking state of Cayor in what is now Senegal. The two men apparently hit it off, for Budomel soon invited Cadamosto to visit his residence about 25 miles inland. Observant and open-minded, Cadamosto later wrote an account of his month-long visit, which has become an important source for historians of fifteenth-century West Africa. In doing so, he also recorded one of the earliest encounters between European explorers and black Africans.

Questions to consider as you examine the source:

■ How would you describe Cadamosto's posture toward Budomel and his society? What did he admire? What did he criticize? In what ways was he judging it by European standards?

■ How might Budomel have written about his encounter with Cadamosto?

■ What could historians learn from this account about this West African society in the mid-fifteenth century? Consider the role of slavery, the position of women, the political system, economic transactions, the penetration of Islam, and relationships with a wider world.

ALVISE DA CADAMOSTO
On Meeting with Budomel
1455

This is what I was able to observe. . . . First, I saw clearly that, though these pass as lords, it must not be thought that they have castles or cities. . . . The King of this realm had nothing save villages of grass huts, and Budomel was lord only of a part of this realm. . . . Such men are not lords by virtue of treasure or money, for they possess neither, but on account of ceremonies and the following of people they may truly be called lords; indeed they receive beyond comparison more obedience than our lords.

The dwelling of such a King is never fixed: he has a number of villages to support his wives and families. In the village where I was, . . . there were from forty to fifty grass huts close together in a circle, surrounded by hedges and groves of great trees, leaving but one or two gaps as entrances. Each hut has a yard divided off by hedges. . . . In this place Budomel had nine wives: and likewise in his other dwellings, according to his will and pleasure. Each of these wives has five or six young negro girls in attendance upon her, and it is as lawful for the lord to sleep with these attendants as with his wives, to whom this does not appear an injury, for it is customary.

These negroes, both men and women, are exceedingly lascivious: Budomel demanded of me importunately, having been given to understand that Christians knew how to do many things, whether by chance I could give him the means by which he could satisfy many women, for which he offered me a great reward.

This Budomel always has at least two hundred negroes with him, who constantly follow him. . . . [T]he nearer one approaches the apartment of Budomel, the greater is the dignity of those living in these courts, up to the door of Budomel.

This Budomel exhibits haughtiness, showing himself only for an hour in the morning, and for a short while towards evening. . . . Such lords as he, when granting audience to anyone, display much ceremony: however considerable he who seeks audience may be, or however high born, on entering the door of Budomel's courtyard he throws himself down on his knees, bows his head to the ground, and with both hands scatters sand upon his naked shoulders and head. . . . No man would be bold enough to come before him to parley, unless he had stripped himself naked save for the girdle of leather they wear.

All this appears to me to proceed from the great fear and dread in which these people hold their lord, since for the most trivial misdeed he seizes and sells their wives and children. Thus it appears to me that his power exacts obedience and fear from the people by selling their wives and children. In two ways they exercise the rights of lords, and display power, that is, in maintaining a train of followers, in allowing themselves to be seen rarely, and in being greatly reverenced by their subjects. . . .

I was permitted to enter the mosque where they pray: arriving towards evening, and having

called those of his . . . Arabs (those who are learned in the laws of Muhammad), he entered with some of his chief lords into a certain place. There they prayed in this fashion: standing upright and frequently looking up to the sky, they took two paces forward, and recited some words in a low voice: then bowed down very often and kissed the earth. . . . And thus they continued for the space of half an hour. [*Note: Cadamosto witnessed the* salat, *the ritual prayer of Islam.*]

When he had finished, he asked me what I thought of it. . . . Finally I told him that his faith was false, and that those who had instructed him in such things were ignorant of the truth. On many grounds I proved his faith to be false and our faith to be true and holy, thus getting the better of his learned men in argument. . . . The lord laughed at this, saying that our faith appeared to him to be good: for it could be no other than God that had bestowed so many good and rich gifts and so much skill and knowledge upon us. . . . He was much pleased with the actions of the Christians, and I am certain it would have been easy to have converted him to the Christian faith, if he had not feared to lose his power.

Each of his wives sends him a certain number of dishes of food every day. All the negro lords and men of this land follow this fashion, their women supplying them with food. They eat on the ground, like animals, without manners. No one eats with these negro rulers, save those Moors [North African Muslims] who teach the law, and one or two of their chief men.

[After learning about a snake-charming ritual], I conclude that all these negroes are great magicians; and others could bear witness to the truth of this charming of the snakes. . . .

I decided to go to see a market. . . . This was held in a field, on Mondays and Fridays. Men and women came to it from the neighbourhood country within a distance of four or five miles, for those who dwelt farther off attended other markets. In this market I perceived quite clearly that these people are exceedingly poor, judging from the wares they brought for sale: that is, cotton, but not in large quantities, cotton thread and cloth, vegetables, oil and millet, wooden bowls, palm leaf mats, and all the other articles they use in their daily life. Men as well as women came to sell, some of the men offering their weapons, and others a little gold, but not in any quantity. They sold everything, item by item, by barter, and not for money, for they have none. They do not use money of any kind, but barter only, one thing for another, two for one, three for two.

These negroes, men and women, crowded to see me as though I were a marvel. It seemed to be a new experience to them to see Christians, whom they had not previously seen. They marvelled no less at my clothing than at my white skin. . . . Some touched my hands and limbs, and rubbed me with their spittle to discover whether my whiteness was dye or flesh. Finding that it was flesh they were astounded.

Horses are highly prized in this country of the Blacks, because they are to be had only with great difficulty, for they are brought from our Barbary [North Africa] by the Arabs and . . . cannot withstand the great heat. A horse with its trappings is sold for from nine to fourteen negro slaves, according to the condition and breeding of the horse. When a chief buys a horse, he sends for his horse-charmers, who have a great fire of certain herbs lighted after their fashion, which makes a great smoke. Into this they lead the horse by the bridle, muttering their spells. . . . Then they fasten to its neck charms [probably containing passages from the Quran]. . . . They believe that with these they are safer in battle.

The women of this country are very pleasant and light-hearted, ready to sing and to dance, especially the young girls. They dance, however, only at night by the light of the moon. Their dances are very different from ours.

These negroes marvelled greatly at many of our possessions, particularly at our crossbows, and, above all, our mortars. Some came to the ship, and I had them shown the firing of a mortar, the noise of which frightened them exceedingly. I then told them that a mortar would slay more than a hundred men at one shot, at which they were astonished, saying that it was an invention of the devil's. . . .

When I had despatched my business, and had acquired a certain number of slaves, I decided to continue beyond Capo Verde, to discover new lands, and to make good my venture.

Source: G. R. Crone, *The Voyages of Cadamosto and Other Documents on Western Africa* (Farnham, Surrey, GBR: Hakluyt Society, 1937), 35–52. Used by permission of the Hakluyt Society.

Source 12.2
Vasco da Gama at Calicut, India

On May 20, 1498, the Portuguese marked a major milestone in over eighty years of voyaging down the west coast of Africa when Vasco da Gama led a small fleet of four ships around the Cape of Good Hope, across the Indian Ocean, arriving at the south Indian port city of Calicut. That event represented the first direct entry of Europeans into the long-established network of Indian Ocean commerce from which they had long obtained precious spices, gemstones, and other luxury goods, albeit only through Muslim intermediaries. Now they were directly operating within this complex, international system of exchange, much of it dominated by Muslims. Commercial desires combined with an anti-Muslim crusading sensibility to fuel Portuguese entry into what was for them another "New World."

When da Gama arrived, the coast of southwestern India hosted a number of small states, cities, and kingdoms, fierce rivals for the rich profits of trade in spices and especially pepper. Calicut, the most prominent of these states, was ruled by Hindus, but Arab Muslims were the most strongly established trading community operating in the city. Both economic interest and religious hostility to Christians ensured that they did not look favorably on the arrival of da Gama.

This initial encounter lasted about three months, much of it recorded in an official journal of da Gama's voyage compiled by an unknown author. Excerpts from the journal provide a flavor of that encounter, obviously from a Portuguese perspective, but "between the lines" we can perhaps discern other perspectives as well.

Questions to consider as you examine the source:

- How might you summarize the motivations and hopes that animated da Gama's voyage? To what extent were they fulfilled?

- How did da Gama explain the difficulties he faced in Calicut? Can you think of other possible explanations for these problems?

- The ruler of Calicut at times seems quite welcoming to da Gama and at other times suspicious and hostile. How might you explain this ambivalence?

A Journal of the First Voyage of Vasco da Gama
1498

[*The first sustained interaction between da Gama and local people occurred in an encounter with two Arab Muslims from Tunis, who could speak Spanish and Italian.*]

The first greeting that he [da Gama] received was in these words: "May the Devil take thee! What brought you hither?" They asked what he sought so far away from home, and he told them that we came in search of Christians and of spices. . . . [One of the Muslims] said these words: "A lucky venture. . . . Plenty of rubies, plenty of emeralds! You owe great thanks to God, for having brought you to a country holding such riches!" We were greatly astonished to hear his talk, for we never expected to hear our language spoken so far away from Portugal. . . .

[*A few days later, da Gama traveled inland for an audience with the ruler of Calicut. The journal notes that* his party observed "many large ships," huge crowds of curious people, and an elaborate "church," most likely a Hindu temple. The Portuguese initially mistook Hindus for Christians, perhaps because they had heard rumors of a small Christian community, allegedly derived from the early missionary work of Saint Thomas, that did in fact live in southern India.]

On landing, the captain-major [da Gama] was received by [an official], with whom were many men, armed and unarmed. The reception was friendly, as if the people were pleased to see us, though at first appearances looked threatening, for they carried naked swords in their hands. A palanquin [a covered chair carried on poles by four men] was provided for the captain-major, such as is used by men of distinction in that country. . . .

The king was in a small court, reclining upon a couch covered with a cloth of green velvet, above which was a good mattress, and upon this again a sheet of cotton stuff, very white and fine. . . . The king . . . asked the captain-major what he wanted. And the captain-major told him he was the ambassador of a King of Portugal, who was Lord of many countries and the possessor of great wealth of every description, exceeding that of any king of these parts; that for a period of sixty years his ancestors had annually sent out vessels to make discoveries in the direction of India, as they knew that there were Christian kings there like themselves. This, he said, was the reason which induced them to order this country to be discovered, not because they sought for gold or silver, for of this they had such abundance that they needed not what was to be found in this country.

[*This visit seemed to go well, but the next day, when da Gama was preparing gifts for the king, several officials came to inspect the gifts.*]

They came, and when they saw the present they laughed at it, saying that it was not a thing to offer to a king, that the poorest merchant from Mecca, or any other part of India, gave more, and that if he wanted to make a present it should be in gold, as the king would not accept such things. . . .

[*The next day, the king kept da Gama waiting for four hours and then belittled Portuguese goods.*]

The king then said that he [da Gama] had told him that he came from a very rich kingdom, and yet had brought him nothing. . . . The king then asked what it was he had come to discover: stones [gems] or men? If he came to discover men, as he said, why had he brought nothing? The king then asked what kind of merchandise was to be found in his country. The captain-major said there was much corn, cloth, iron, bronze, and many other things. The king asked whether he had any merchandise with him. The captain-major replied that he had a little of each sort, as samples, and that if permitted to return to the ships he would order it to be landed. . . . The king said no! He might take all his people with him, securely moor his ships, land his merchandise, and sell it to the best advantage [in the private market]. . . . [But even in this private trading], we did not, however, effect these sales at the prices hoped for when we arrived . . . , for a very fine shirt which in Portugal fetches 300 reis, was worth here only 30 reis. And just as we sold shirts cheaply so we sold other things, in order to take some things away from this country, if only for samples. Those who visited the city bought there cloves, cinnamon, and precious stones.

[*The Portuguese had little doubt as to the source of this apparent hostility.*]

We also felt grieved that a Christian [actually a Hindu] king, to whom we had given of ours, should do us such an ill turn. At the same time we did not hold him as culpable as he seemed to be, for we were well aware that the Moors [Muslims] of the place, who were merchants from Mecca and elsewhere, could ill digest us. They had told the king that we were thieves, and that if once we navigated to his country, no more ships from Mecca, nor . . . any other part, would visit him. They added that he would derive no profit from this [trade with Portugal] as we had nothing to give, but would rather take away, and that thus his country would be ruined. They, moreover, offered rich bribes to the king to capture and kill us, so that we should not return to Portugal.

[*What followed was a series of controversies about the unloading of da Gama's ships, the mutual seizure of hostages, the payment required before leaving Calicut, and more. Several minor naval engagements showed da Gama that even if his goods were not so appealing, his on-board artillery far surpassed anything available locally. When he arrived home, da Gama found a very pleased king of Portugal, who wrote with pleasure to the monarchs of Spain about da Gama's achievement.*]

[W]e learn that they did reach and discover India and other kingdoms and lordships bordering upon it; that they entered and navigated its sea, finding large cities, large edifices and rivers, and great populations, among whom is carried on all the trade in spices and precious stones, which are forwarded in ships . . . to Mecca, and thence to Cairo, whence they are dispersed throughout the world. Of these [spices, etc.] they have brought a quantity, including cinnamon, cloves, ginger, nutmeg, and pepper as well as other kinds, together with the boughs and leaves of the same; also many fine stones of all sorts, such as rubies and others.

And they also came to a country in which there are mines of gold. . . .

[W]hat we have learnt concerning the Christian people whom these explorers reached [is] that it will be possible, notwithstanding that they are not as yet strong in the faith or possessed of a thorough knowledge of it, to do much in the service of God and the exaltation of the Holy Faith, once they shall have been converted and fully fortified (confirmed) in it. And when they shall have thus been fortified in the faith there will be an opportunity for destroying the Moors of those parts. Moreover we hope, with the help of God that the great trade which now enriches the Moors of those parts . . . , shall, in consequence of our regulations, be diverted to the natives and ships of our own kingdom.

Source: E. G. Ravenstein, trans., *A Journal of the First Voyage of Vasco da Gama, 1497–1499* (London: Hakluyt Society, 1898), https://openlibrary.org/books/OL6912713M/A_journal_of_the_first_voyage_of_Vasco_da_Gama_1497-1499.

Source 12.3
Celebrating da Gama's Arrival in Calicut

The extraordinary feats of navigation accomplished by Portuguese sailors gave their kingdom a new prominence on the European stage. Portuguese rulers publicized their accomplishments by displaying the exotic products from the East to a European public hungry for information about distant lands. Perhaps no single item brought back from India created a greater stir than the live rhinoceros that arrived in 1515. Crowds flocked in amazement to view a beast that had not been seen in Europe for over 1,000 years and was only known through an account by the ancient Roman scholar Pliny.

The most systematic effort to associate the Portuguese monarchy with the opening of the East took the form of a twenty-six-panel series of tapestries commemorating da Gama's 1498 voyage to Calicut. Commissioned by King Manuel in 1504, these expensive woven works of art were intended to hang in the great hall of the royal palace where official business was conducted. The scenes incorporate a wide variety of exotica, including dark-skinned people dressed in elaborate, if often inaccurate, costumes and rare or mythical animals. Woven in the Low Countries (modern day Belgium and the Netherlands), by artisans who had never seen their subjects, the tapestries feature many scenes containing fanciful elements, while other scenes draw on more familiar topics, including classical accounts of Alexander the Great's conquests in the East. Nevertheless, these tapestries proved influential in shaping European conceptions of India, as the same artisans produced many copies and variations on these panels for other European elites fascinated by the Portuguese discoveries.

The panel reproduced here depicts the arrival of da Gama at Calicut. The scene includes accurate renderings of Portuguese vessels anchored in the port; however, the buildings and town gates of Calicut are more fanciful, constructed out of distinctly European, not Indian, architectural elements. In the foreground to the left, da Gama presents a letter from his monarch to the ruler of Calicut. In the center of the scene, the Portuguese are in the process of unloading from their vessels exotic animals, including ostriches, wild cats, and even a unicorn. To the right, a great crowd dressed in garments reminiscent of European styles gathers to view these curiosities, very much like the Europeans who gathered to view the Indian rhinoceros unloaded in Lisbon harbor in 1515.

Questions to consider as you examine the source:

■ In what ways does this image reflect the written account in Source 12.2? In what ways does it differ?

■ How does this tapestry serve the purposes of King Manuel of Portugal, who commissioned it?

■ What can you discern about European knowledge of India from this image?

The Arrival of da Gama at Calicut

Museu Nacional de Arte Antiga, Lisbon, Portugal/Alfred Dagli Orti/Art Resource, NY

Source 12.4
Columbus in the Caribbean

Even apart from its horrific long-term consequences, Columbus's arrival in the Caribbean region in October of 1492 retains a distinctive significance. Europeans were at least aware of Asian and African societies and had experienced some interaction, often indirect, with them. But except for the brief and unremembered incursions of the Vikings, no one from the Afro-Eurasian hemisphere had set foot in the Americas since the last migrants from Siberia had crossed the Bering Strait perhaps 15,000 years earlier. So the arrival of Columbus was an extraordinary encounter.

Columbus's voyage, sponsored by the monarchs of Spain, found a densely settled agricultural people known as the Taino inhabiting the islands now called Hispaniola (modern Haiti and Dominican Republic), Cuba, Jamaica, and Puerto Rico. Organized into substantial village communities governed by a hierarchy of chiefs (*cacique*), Taino society featured modest class distinctions. An elite group of chiefs, warriors, artists, and religious specialists enjoyed a higher status than did commoners, who worked the fields, fished, and hunted.

On the voyage back to Europe in early 1493, Columbus penned a letter to Lord Raphael Sanchez, a prominent official in the government of his patrons, King Ferdinand and Queen Isabella of Spain. In it he summarized his initial impressions and his hopes for the future for both Sanchez and his royal patrons.

Questions to consider as you examine the source:

■ What can you infer from the letter about Columbus's expectations for his journey and what he wanted from his Spanish patrons?

■ Scholars have noted a number of omissions from Columbus's letter: that one of his ships had been lost; that some of his men had abused local women; that he had had at least one violent encounter with local people; that his ability to communicate with the Taino was minimal. Why might he have omitted these incidents?

■ How might you summarize Columbus's posture toward the people he met on this first voyage? Can you see ways in which he was trying to "spin" his description of these people? Did he have preconceptions that may have colored his understanding of them?

CHRISTOPHER COLUMBUS
Letter to Ferdinand and Isabella
1493

Thirty-three days after my departure from Cadiz [in Spain] I reached the Indian [Caribbean] sea, where I discovered many islands, thickly peopled, of which I took possession without resistance in the name of our most illustrious Monarch, by public proclamation and with unfurled banners . . . ; to each of these I also gave a name, ordering that one should be called Santa Maria de la Concepcion, another Fernandina, the third Isabella, the fourth Juana, and so with all the rest respectively.

As soon as we arrived at Juana, I proceeded along its coast a short distance. . . . I could not suppose it to be an island, but the continental province of Cathay [China]. Seeing, however, no towns or populous places on the sea coast, but only a few detached houses and cottages, with whose inhabitants I was unable to communicate, because they fled as soon as they saw us, I went further on, thinking that in my progress I should certainly find some city or village. . . . I afterwards dispatched two of our men to ascertain whether there were a king or any cities in that province. These men reconnoitered the country for three days, and found a most numerous population, and great numbers of houses, though small, and built without any regard to order. . . .

The inhabitants of both sexes in this island, and in all the others which I have seen, go always naked as they were born, with the exception of some of the women, who use the covering of a leaf, or small bough, or an apron of cotton. . . . None of them . . . are possessed of any iron, neither have they weapons, being unacquainted with, and indeed incompetent to use them, not from any deformity of body (for they are well-formed), but because they are timid and full of fear. . . . This timidity did not arise from any loss or injury that they had received from us; for, on the contrary, I gave to all I approached whatever articles I had about me, such as cloth and many other things,

taking nothing of theirs in return. . . . As soon however as they see that they are safe, and have laid aside all fear, they are very simple and honest, and exceedingly liberal with all they have; none of them refusing anything he may possess when he is asked for it, but on the contrary inviting us to ask them. They exhibit great love towards all others in preference to themselves: they also give objects of great value for trifles. . . .

Thus they bartered, like idiots, cotton and gold for fragments of bows, glasses, bottles, and jars; which I forbad as being unjust, and myself gave them many beautiful and acceptable articles which I had brought with me, taking nothing from them in return; I did this in order that I might the more easily conciliate them, that they might be led to become Christians, and be inclined to entertain a regard for the King and Queen, our Princes and all Spaniards, and that I might induce them to take an interest in seeking out, and collecting, and delivering to us such things as they possessed in abundance, but which we greatly needed.

They practice no kind of idolatry, but have a firm belief that all strength and power, and indeed all good things, are in heaven, and that I had descended from thence with these ships and sailors, and under this impression was I received after they had thrown aside their fears. Nor are they slow or stupid, but of very clear understanding; and those men who have crossed to the neighbouring islands give an admirable description of everything they observed; but they never saw any people clothed, nor any ships like ours.

On my arrival at that sea, I had taken some Indians by force from the first island that I came to, in order that they might learn our language, and communicate to us what they knew respecting the country; which plan succeeded excellently, and was a great advantage to us, for in a short time, either by gestures and signs, or by words, we were enabled to understand each other.

Each of these islands has a great number of canoes, built of solid wood, narrow. . . . These canoes are of various sizes, but the greater number are constructed with eighteen banks of oars, and with these they cross to the other islands. . . . I took possession of all these islands in the name of our invincible King, yet there was one large town in Espanola of which especially I took possession, situated . . . in every way convenient for the purposes of gain and commerce.

To this town I gave the name of Navidad del Senor, and ordered a fortress to be built there, I also . . . engaged the favor and friendship of the King of the island . . . , for these people are so amiable and friendly that even the King took a pride in calling me his brother. . . . [T]hose who hold the said fortress, can easily keep the whole island in check, without any pressing danger to themselves. . . .

As far as I have learned, every man throughout these islands is united to but one wife, with the exception of the kings and princes, who are allowed to have twenty: the women seem to work more than the men. I could not clearly understand whether the people possess any private property, for I observed that one man had the charge of distributing various things to the rest, but especially meat and provisions and the like. . . .

[I]n a certain island called Charis . . . dwell a people who are considered by the neighbouring islanders as most ferocious: and these feed upon human flesh. The same people have many kinds of canoes, in which they cross to all the surrounding islands and rob and plunder wherever they can. . . . These are the men who form unions with certain women, who dwell alone in the island Matenin, which lies next to Espanola on the side towards India; these latter [women] employ themselves in no labour suitable to their own sex, for they use bows and javelins as I have already described their paramours as doing. . . .

I promise, that with a little assistance afforded me by our most invincible sovereigns, I will procure them as much gold as they need, as great a quantity of spices, of cotton, and of mastic . . . , and as many men [slaves] for the service of the navy as their Majesties may require. I promise also rhubarb and other sorts of drugs. . . . Although all I have related may appear to be wonderful and unheard of, yet the results of my voyage would have been more astonishing if I had had at my disposal such ships as I required. But these great and marvellous results are not to be attributed to any merit of mine, but to the holy Christian faith, and to the piety and religion of our Sovereigns. . . . Thus it has happened to me in the present instance, who have accomplished a task to which the powers of mortal men had never hitherto attained.

Source: Christopher Columbus, letter to Lord Raphael Sanchez (treasurer to Ferdinand and Isabella), 14 March 1493, The Internet Modern History Sourcebook, Fordham University, accessed June 1, 2015, http://www2.fiu.edu/~harveyb/colum.html.

Source 12.5
Columbus Engraved

Precisely a century after Columbus first arrived in the Americas, the Flemish artist Theodore de Bry depicted his landing in an engraving that has become an iconic image of that event. While some elements of the engraving are accurate, including the ships, the raising of a cross, and the dress of Columbus's men, others are fanciful, like the jewelry, ornate vessels, and chests, all made of gold and in European Renaissance styles, that the Taino offer Columbus.

Questions to consider as you examine the source:

■ How does de Bry portray Columbus's assertion of authority in a land so far from his own?

■ How does the artist differentiate between the Europeans and the Taino?

■ How would you summarize the "message" of this image?

Columbus Arriving on Hispaniola

From *Americae Tertia Pars IV*, 1594/bpk, Berlin/Art Resource, NY

ESSAY QUESTIONS

Early Encounters; First Impressions

1. **Comparing first encounters:** How would you compare the first impressions that these three encounters generated for the Europeans involved? What surprised them? What offended their sensibilities? How did they describe or portray cultural differences? How open to these differences did they seem to be?

2. **Establishing political ties:** What political relationship with the host society did each of the Europeans have? What were they seeking from those societies? To what extent did these factors shape their posture toward those they were meeting for the first time?

3. **Reading between the lines:** Although these sources all derive from Europeans, what might we infer, reading between the lines, about how the West African, Indian, and Native American figures may have understood these encounters?

4. **Foreshadowing future encounters:** In what ways did these encounters bear the seeds of future developments, although unknown to everyone at the time?

Source 10.4
Jerusalem and the Crusades

As a city sacred to Christians, Jews, and Muslims alike, Jerusalem lay at the epicenter of the Crusades. Two images of the city, both painted by European artists in the fifteenth century to adorn richly decorated books, portray two decisive events of the Crusades. The first shows the Christian seizure of Jerusalem in 1099, while the second records Saladin's retaking of the city in 1187. While the subject matter of the two images is historical, the depictions of Jerusalem are fanciful, incorporating Western European architectural features such as European fortifications and houses. Painted centuries after the event, these images provide evidence of how Europeans perceived the Crusades after their conclusion.

Questions to consider as you examine the source:

■ What is happening in each of the paintings?

■ Saladin is that rare Muslim figure who achieved a heroic stature in both the Christian and Islamic worlds. Why might the artist who painted the image in Source 10.4B have portrayed Saladin in such a positive light?

■ To what extent do these paintings illustrate al-Athir's account of these two events?

■ Based on Urban II's speech in Source 10.1, would he have been pleased with or appalled at the behavior shown in Source 10.4A?

Source 10.4A
The Looting of Jerusalem
1099

Source 10.4B
How Jerusalem Was Captured by Saladin
1187

Source 10.5
A Byzantine Perspective on the Crusades

The Crusades began in an effort by Pope Urban II to reconcile long-standing tensions between the Eastern and Western Churches by coming to the aid of a Byzantine Empire beleaguered by Muslim armies. Precisely the opposite actually occurred, as even a common hostility to Islam failed to overcome those differences. Mutual distrust and some violence between Roman Catholic and Eastern Orthodox Christians came to a climax in 1204, when Crusaders on their way to Egypt diverted to Constantinople and sacked the city. In an emotional eyewitness account, the Byzantine official and historian Nicetas Choniates described that event, which solidified the hostility between these two branches of Christendom.

Questions to consider as you examine the source:

- How does this passage characterize the Crusaders?

- How does the sense of violation expressed in this passage compare with that of Pope Urban II in Source 10.1 and the Muslim historians in Source 10.3? What common features can you discern?

- How do you think this event affected the possibility of reconciliation between the Eastern and Western Churches?

NICETAS CHONIATES
The Sack of Constantinople
1204

How shall I begin to tell of the deeds wrought by these nefarious men! Alas, the images, which ought to have been adored, were trodden under foot! Alas, the relics of the holy martyrs were thrown into unclean places! . . . [T]he divine body and blood of Christ was spilled upon the ground or thrown about. They snatched the precious reliquaries [containers for sacred relics], thrust into their bosoms the ornaments which these contained, and used the broken remnants for pans and drinking cups, precursors of Anti-Christ. . . .

Nor can the violation of the Great Church [Hagia Sophia] be listened to with equanimity. For the sacred altar was broken into bits and distributed among the soldiers, as was all the other sacred wealth of so great and infinite splendor.

When the sacred vases and utensils of unsurpassable art and grace and rare material, and the fine silver, wrought with gold . . . were to be borne away as booty, mules and saddled horses were led to the very sanctuary of the temple. Some of these which were unable to keep their footing on the splendid and slippery pavement, were stabbed when they fell, so that the sacred pavement was polluted with blood and filth.

Nay more, a certain harlot, a sharer in their guilt . . . , a servant of the demons, a worker of incantations and poisonings, insulting Christ, sat in the patriarch's seat, singing an obscene song and dancing frequently. Could those, who showed so great madness against God Himself, have spared the honorable matrons and maidens or the virgins consecrated to God?

Nothing was more difficult and laborious than to soften by prayers, to render benevolent, these wrathful barbarians, vomiting forth bile at every unpleasing word, so that nothing failed to inflame their fury. . . . Often they drew their daggers against anyone who opposed them at all or hindered their demands.

No one was without a share in the grief. In the alleys, in the streets, in the temples, complaints, weeping, lamentations, grief, the groaning of men, the shrieks of women, wounds, rape, captivity, the separation of those most closely united. Nobles wandered about ignominiously, those of venerable age in tears, the rich in poverty. Thus it was in the streets, on the corners, in the temple, in the dens, for no place remained unassailed or defended the suppliants.

Source: D. C. Munro, trans., *Translations and Reprints from the Original Sources of European History*, series 1, vol. 3:1, rev. ed. (Philadelphia: University of Pennsylvania Press, 1912), 15–16.

Source 10.6
More Than Conflict

The Crusades have long been seen as an arena of conflict between Christians and Muslims with violence and brutality on both sides. And yet at least on occasion it is possible to witness something more than this. Trade between Christians and Muslims persisted, and they rented property to one another. The mid-twelfth-century Muslim writer Ibn al-Qaysrani penned celebratory poems about the churches of the Crusader city of Antioch, the beauty of Greek Orthodox church liturgy, and the loveliness of Frankish women. A Muslim warrior named Usmah Ibn Munqidh (1095–1188), who had fought the Crusaders with Saladin, wrote of a Frankish knight who called him "brother." "Between us," Usmah Ibn Munqidh declared, "were mutual bonds of amity and friendship." In the first selection below, Usmah, who elsewhere wrote of Europeans in highly negative terms, described his encounter with a group of Christian monks.

Questions to consider as you examine the source:

■ What did he find surprising about this encounter?

■ Why was he initially disappointed?

■ What does his comment about the Sufis reveal about his posture to the Christians?

Source 10.6A
Usmah Ibn Munqidh

Christian Piety and Muslim Piety
Mid-Twelfth Century

I paid a visit to the tomb of John [the Baptist in Damascus]. . . . After saying my prayers . . . I entered a church. Inside were about ten old men, their bare heads as white as combed cotton. They were facing east. . . . They gave hospitality to those who needed it. The sight of their piety touched my heart, but at the same time it displeased and saddened me, for I had never seen such zeal and devotion among the Muslims. For some time I brooded on this experience, until one day, as Mu'in ad-Din and I were passing the Peacock House . . . we dismounted and went into a long building set at an angle to the road. For the moment I thought there was no one there. Then I saw about a hundred prayer mats, and on each a sufi, his face expressing peaceful serenity, and his body humble devotion. This was a reassuring sight, and I gave thanks to Almighty God that there were among the Muslims men of even more zealous devotion than those Christian priests. Before this I had never seen sufis in their monastery, and was ignorant of the way they lived.

Source: *Arab Historians of the Crusades*, edited and translated by Francesco Gabrieli, © 1996 by Routledge and Kegan Paul Ltd. Published by the University of California Press. Used by permission of the University of California Press and by permission of Taylor & Francis Books UK.

Source 10.6B
Fulcher of Chartres

The Latins in the East
Early Twelfth Century

In this next passage, a French priest, Fulcher of Chartres, who accompanied the First Crusade to Jerusalem and lived there until 1127, wrote about Europeans who had settled permanently in one of the Crusader states.

Questions to consider as you examine the source:

- According to Fulcher, what was happening to Europeans who lived in the Holy Land for some time?

- How does he explain this transformation?

- What limits to assimilation are suggested in this passage?

Consider, I pray, and reflect how in our time God has transferred the West into the East, for we who were Occidentals now have been made Orientals. He who was a Roman or a Frank is now a Galilaean, or an inhabitant of Palestine. One who was a citizen of Rheims or of Chartres now has been made a citizen of Tyre or of Antioch. We have already forgotten the places of our birth; already they have become unknown to many of us, or, at least, are unmentioned. Some already possess here homes and servants which they have received through inheritance. Some have taken wives not merely of their own people, but Syrians, or Armenians, or even Saracens [Muslims] who have received the grace of baptism. . . . There are here, too, grandchildren and great-grandchildren. . . . Different languages, now made common, become known to both races, and faith unites those whose forefathers were strangers. . . . For those who were poor there, here God makes rich . . . and those who had not had a villa, here, by the gift of God, already possess a city. Therefore why should one who has found the East so favorable return to the West?

Source: August C. Krey, *The First Crusade: The Accounts of Eye-Witnesses and Participants* (Princeton, NJ: Princeton University Press, 1921), 280–81.

ESSAY QUESTIONS

The Crusades as Cultural Encounter

1. **Reflecting on religious world views:** It may be difficult for modern Westerners to fully grasp how extensively religion shaped the worldview of people in earlier times. In what ways do these sources reveal such a religiously based outlook on life? How was occupation by armies bearing an alien religion actually experienced?

2. **Interacting with other religions:** To what extent was the posture of European Crusaders toward Muslims, Jews, and Eastern Christians similar? Do you notice any differences?

3. **Considering point of view:** Which of the outcomes of the Crusades would have been pleasing to Urban II? Which would have disappointed or appalled him?

4. **Conceiving the "other":** To what extent did these sources exhibit any genuine understanding of other people? Did they show any nuance in their portrayal of the "other"? Or given the conditions of the Crusades, is this too much to ask?

Note

1. Carol Hillenbrand, *The Crusades: Islamic Perspectives* (New York: Routledge, 2000), chap. 5. The quote is on page 274.

CHAPTER 11

THINKING THROUGH SOURCES

Living and Dying during the Black Death

Among the most far-reaching outcomes of the Mongol moment in world history was the spread all across Asia, the Middle East, Europe, and North Africa of that deadly disease known as the plague or the Black Death. While the Mongols certainly did not cause the plague, their empire facilitated the movement not only of goods and people but also of the microorganisms responsible for this pestilence. Its sudden arrival in the late 1340s, the enormity of its death toll, the social trauma it generated, the absence of any remembered frame of reference for an event so devastating — all of this left people everywhere bewildered, imagining the end of the world. The sources that follow illustrate how people in various cultural settings experienced this initial phase of the catastrophe, sought to understand what was happening, and tried to cope with it. This exercise begins with three general accounts of the arrival of the plague — in the Islamic Middle East, Western Europe, and the Byzantine Empire — followed by five sources that focus on more specific aspects of this hemispheric pandemic.

Source 11.1
The Black Death in the Islamic World

Ibn al-Wardi was an Arab Muslim writer living in Aleppo, Syria, when the plague struck. He wrote extensively about what he witnessed and then died from the pestilence in 1349. As the only major contemporary account of the Black Death to survive from the Middle East, it was widely quoted by later Muslim writers and remains a major source for modern historians. His account is thoroughly informed by an Islamic religious sensibility, especially when he refers to the "noble tradition" that prohibits fleeing an outbreak of disease. Three passages from the hadiths, sayings attributed to Muhammad, were especially important:

> When you learn that epidemic disease exists in a country, do not go there, but if it breaks out in the country where you are, do not leave.

> He who dies of epidemic disease is a martyr.

It is a punishment that God inflicts on whom he wills, but He has granted a modicum of clemency with respect to Believers.[1]

These teachings made it a matter of faith for many Muslims to trust in God to protect them from the plague.

Questions to consider as you examine the source:

■ How does Ibn al-Wardi seek to explain the plague?

■ What does this document reveal about the range of initial responses to it?

■ In what ways does Islam inform Ibn al-Wardi's account of these events?

IBN AL-WARDI

Report of the Pestilence
1348

The plague frightened and killed. It began in the land of darkness [Northern Asia]. Oh, what a visitor! . . . China was not preserved from it. The plague afflicted the Indians in India. . . . It attacked the Persians . . . and gnawed away at the Crimea. . . . The plague destroyed mankind in Cairo . . . the scourge came to Jerusalem. . . . It overtook those people who fled to the al-Aqsa Mosque. . . .

How amazingly does it pursue the people of each house. One of them spits blood and everyone in the household is certain of death . . . after two or three nights.

Oh God, it is acting by your command. Lift this from us.

The pestilence caused the people of Aleppo the same disturbance. . . . Oh, if you could see the nobles of Aleppo studying their inscrutable books of medicine. They multiply its remedies by eating dried and sour food. . . . They perfumed their homes with ambergris and camphor. . . . They wore ruby rings and put onions, vinegar, and sardines together with the daily meal. . . .

If you see many biers and their carriers and hear in every quarter of Aleppo the announcements of death and cries, you run from them and refuse to stay with them. The profits of the undertakers have greatly increased. . . . Those who sweat from carrying coffins enjoy this plague-time.

We ask God's forgiveness for our souls' bad inclinations; the plague is surely part of His punishment.

The plague is for the Muslims a martyrdom and a reward, and for the disbelievers a punishment and a rebuke. . . . It has been established by our Prophet . . . that the plague-stricken are martyrs. . . . And this secret should be pleasing to the true believer. If someone says that it causes infection and destruction, say: God creates and recreates. . . . If we acknowledge the plague's devastation of the people, it is the will of the Chosen Doer. I take refuge in God from the yoke of the plague.

One man begs another to take care of his children, and one says goodbye to his neighbors. A third perfects his work, and another prepares his shroud. A fifth is reconciled with his enemies, and another treats his friends with kindness. . . . One man puts aside his property [in a religious endowment called a *waqf*]; one frees his servants. One man changes his character, while another amends his ways. There is no protection today from it other than His mercy, praise be to God.

Nothing prevented us from running away from the plague, except our devotion to the noble tradition [prohibiting flight from a plague-stricken land]. Come then, seek the aid of God Almighty for raising the plague, for He is the best helper. . . .

We do not depend on our good health against the plague, but on You [God].

[*Somewhat later, a fifteenth-century account of the plague in Cairo by the Egyptian scholar al-Maqrizi reported that people received very high wages for reciting the Quran at funerals, caring for the ill, and washing the dead. Many trades disappeared as artisans found more lucrative employment in plague-related occupations. Fields went unharvested for lack of peasants to do the work. Weddings and family feasts vanished, and even the call to prayer was sometimes canceled. Al-Maqrizi* reported that in Cairo, "*some people appropriated for themselves without scruple the immovable and movable goods and cash of their former owners after their demise. But very few lived long enough to profit thereby.*"[2]]

Source: Michael Dols, "Ibn al-Wardi's Risalah al-Naba' 'an al-Waba', a Translation of a Major Source for the History of the Black Death in the Middle East" in *Near Eastern Numismatics, Iconography, Epigraphy and History: Studies in Honor of George C. Miles*, ed. Dickran K. Kouymjian (Beirut: American University of Beirut, 1974), 448–455. Reprinted by permission of the American University of Beirut Press.

Source 11.2
The Black Death in Western Europe

Like Ibn al-Wardi in Aleppo, the Italian writer Giovanni Boccaccio of Florence, Italy, was an eyewitness to the plague in his city. He recorded his impressions of the plague, which claimed the lives of his father and stepmother, in a preface to *The Decameron*, completed around 1353. That fictional collection of tales was set in a villa outside Florence, where a group of seven women and three men took turns telling stories to one another while escaping the plague that was ravaging their city.

Questions to consider as you examine the source:

- How does Boccaccio describe the social breakdown that accompanied the plague in Florence?
- What different responses to the plague does he identify?
- In what ways does Boccaccio's account overlap with that of Ibn al-Wardi? And how does it differ?

GIOVANNI BOCCACCIO
The Decameron
Mid-Fourteenth Century

[In 1348] into the distinguished city of Florence . . . there came a deadly pestilence. . . . And against this pestilence no human wisdom or foresight was of any avail; quantities of filth were removed from the city by officials. . . . [T]he entry of any sick person into the city was prohibited; and many directives were issued concerning the maintenance of good health. Nor were the humble supplications, rendered not once but many times by the pious to God, through public processions or by other means, in any way efficacious.

Neither a doctor's advice nor the strength of medicine could do anything to cure this illness; . . . in fact, the number of doctors, other than the well-trained, was increased by a large number of men and women who had never had any medical training; at any rate, few of the sick were ever cured, and almost all died after the third day of the appearance of the previously described symptoms. . . .

There came about such a fear and such fantastic notions among those who remained alive that almost all of them took a very cruel attitude in the matter; that is, they completely avoided the sick and their possessions, and in so doing, each one believed that he was protecting his own good health.

There were some people who thought that living moderately and avoiding any excess might help a great deal in resisting this disease, and so they gathered in small groups and lived entirely apart from everyone else. . . . Allowing no one to speak about or listen to anything said about the sick and the dead outside, these people lived, entertaining themselves with music and other pleasures that they could arrange.

Others thought the opposite: they believed that drinking excessively, enjoying life, going about singing and celebrating, satisfying in every way the appetites as best one could, laughing and making light of everything that happened was the best medicine for such a disease; so they practiced to the fullest what they believed by going from one tavern to another all day and night, drinking to excess; and they would often make merry in private homes, doing everything that pleased or amused them the most. This they were able to do easily for everyone felt he was doomed to die and as a result abandoned his property, so that most of the houses had become common property, and any stranger who came upon them used them as if he were their rightful owner. . . .

And in this great affliction and misery of our city the revered authority of the laws, both divine and human, had fallen and almost completely disappeared, for, like other men, the ministers and executors of the laws were either dead or sick. . . . As a result, everybody was free to do as he pleased.

Others . . . maintained that there was no better medicine against the plague than to flee from it. . . . [M]en and women in great numbers abandoned their city, their houses, their farms, their relatives, and their possessions and sought other places, going at least as far away as the Florentine countryside. . . . [B]rother abandoned brother, uncle abandoned nephew, sister left brother, and very often wife abandoned husband, and — even worse, almost unbelievable — fathers and mothers neglected to tend and care for their children as if they were not their own. . . .

When a woman fell sick, no matter how attractive or beautiful or noble she might be, she did not mind having a manservant (whoever he might be, no matter how young or old he was), and she had no shame whatsoever in revealing any part of her body to him . . . when necessity of her sickness required her to do so. This practice was, perhaps, in the days that followed the pestilence, the cause of looser morals in the women who survived the plague. . . .

With the fury of the pestilence increasing, [traditional burial customs] for the most part died out and other practices took [their] place . . . so not only did people die without having a number of women around them, but there were many who passed away without having even a single witness present. . . . And these dead bodies were not even carried on the shoulders of honored and reputable citizens but rather by gravediggers from the lower classes that were called *becchini*. Working for pay, they would pick up the bier and hurry it off. . . .

Many ended their lives in public streets, during the day or at night. . . . The city was full of corpses. . . . So many corpses would arrive in front of the church every day and at every hour that the amount of holy ground for burials was certainly insufficient for the ancient customs of giving each body its individual place; when all the graves were full, huge trenches were dug in all of the cemeteries of the churches and into them the new arrivals were dumped by the hundreds; and they were packed in there with dirt, one on top of another, like ship's cargo. . . .

But . . . the hostile winds blowing there did not . . . spare the surrounding countryside. . . . In the scattered villages and in the fields the poor, miserable peasants and their families without any medical assistance or aid of servants, died on the roads and in their fields and homes, as many by day as by night, and they died not like men but more like animals. . . . When they saw that death was upon them, completely neglecting the future fruits of their past labors, their livestock, their property, they did their best to consume what they already had to hand. So it came about that oxen, donkeys, sheep, pigs, chickens, and even dogs, man's most faithful companion, were driven from their homes into the fields where the wheat was left not only unharvested but also unreaped, and they were allowed to roam where they wished. . . .

So great was the cruelty of Heaven, and, perhaps, also that of man, that from March to July of the same year, between the fury of the pestiferous sickness and the fact that many of the sick were badly treated or abandoned in need because of the fear that the healthy had, more than one hundred thousand human beings are believed to have lost their lives for certain inside the walls of the city of Florence.

Source 11.3
The Black Death in Byzantium

In 1347, the plague struck Constantinople, capital of the Byzantine Empire, and quickly touched the royal family, as the young son of Emperor John VI and Empress Irene perished from the disease. Eight years later, the emperor abdicated his throne, retiring to a monastery, where he wrote a history of the Byzantine Empire. That work contained a description of the plague as it arrived in Constantinople.

Questions to consider as you examine the source:

- In what larger context did Emperor John VI place the plague and his own personal tragedy?

- How did Emperor John VI describe the outcomes of the plague?

- Does this account have more in common with that of Ibn al-Wardi or Boccaccio?

EMPEROR JOHN VI OF BYZANTIUM
Historarum
Mid- to Late Fourteenth Century

Upon arrival in Byzantium, she [the empress Irene] found Andronikos, the youngest born, dead from the invading plague. . . . [It has] spread throughout almost the entire world.

So incurable was the evil that neither any regularity of life, nor any bodily strength could resist it. Strong and weak bodies were all similarly carried away and those best cared for died in the same manner as the poor. . . . Neither did the disease take the same course in all persons.

Great abscesses were formed on the legs or the arms, from which, when cut, a large quantity of foul-smelling pus flowed. . . . Even many who were seized by all the symptoms unexpectedly recovered. There was no help from anywhere; if someone brought to another a remedy useful to himself, this became poison to the other patient. Some, by treating others, became infected with the disease.

It caused great destruction and many homes were deserted by their inhabitants. Domestic animals died together with their masters. Most terrible was the discouragement. Whenever people felt sick there was hope left for recovery, but by turning to despair, adding to their prostration and severely aggravating their sickness, they died at once.

No words could express the nature of the disease. All that can be pointed out is that it had nothing in common with the everyday evils to which the nature of man is subject, but was something else sent by God to restore chastity. [Many of the sick turned to better things in their minds, by being chastened, not only those who died, but also those who overcame the disease.] They abstained from all vice during that time and they lived virtuously; many divided their property among the poor, even before they were attacked by the disease. If he ever felt himself seized, no one was so ruthless as not to show repentance of his faults and to appear before the judgment seat of God with the best chance of salvation, not believing that the soul was incurable or unhealed.

Many died in Byzantium then, and the king's son, Andronikos, was attacked and died the third day.

Source: Christos S. Bartsocas, "Two Fourteenth-Century Descriptions of the 'Black Death,'" *Journal of the History of Medicine and Allied Sciences* by YALE UNIVERSITY. Reproduced with permission of OXFORD UNIVERSITY PRESS in the format reuse in a book/e-book via Copyright Clearance Center.

Source 11.4
Religious Responses in the Islamic World

Religion permeated the worlds of both Islam and Christianity during the fourteenth century. It is hardly surprising, then, that many people would turn to religious practices in their efforts to understand and cope with a catastrophe of such immense proportions. And yet for a few, the plague challenged established religious understandings. Some Islamic scholars had long opposed the idea of contagion as an explanation for the spread of disease as it seemed to grant human actions, rather than God's decree, the primary role in this process. The plague, however, persuaded one Muslim scholar and physician, al-Khatib, to reject this teaching. "The existence of contagion," he wrote, "has been proved by experience, deduction, the senses, observation, and by unanimous reports."[3]

Most people, however, turned to traditional religious practices to find some sense of meaning, comfort, and protection in the face of the unimaginable tragedy. Source 10.4, written by Ibn Kathir, an Islamic teacher from Damascus, describes one such event.

Questions to consider as you examine the source:

■ What specific practices did the Muslims of Damascus undertake? Why might they have chanted the Quran's account of the flood of Noah in particular?

■ What assumptions underlay these practices?

■ What might you infer from Ibn Kathir's description of the composition of the gathered crowd?

IBN KATHIR
The Beginning and the End: On History
ca. 1350–1351

At Damascus, a reading of the *Traditions* of Bukhari [a collection of the sayings of Muhammad] took place on June 5 of this year [1348] after the public prayer — with the great magistrates there assisting in the presence of a very dense crowd. The ceremony continued with a recitation of a section of the Koran, and the people poured out their supplication that the city be spared the plague. . . . It was predicted and feared that it would become a menace to Damascus. . . . On the morning of June 7, the crowd reassembled . . . and resumed the recitation of the flood of Noah. . . . During this month, the mortality increased among the population of Damascus, until it reached a daily average of more than 100 persons.

On Monday July 21, a proclamation made in the city invited the population to fast for three day; they were further asked to go on the fourth day, a Friday, to the Mosque of the Foot in order to humbly beseech God to take away this plague. . . . On the morning of July 25, the inhabitants threw themselves [into these ceremonies] at every opportunity. . . . One saw in this multitude Jews, Christians, Samaritans, old men, old women, young children, poor men, emirs, notables, magistrates, who processed after the morning prayer, not ceasing to chant their prayers until daybreak. That was a memorable ceremony. . . .

[By October] in the environs of the capital, the dead were innumerable, a thousand in a few days.

Source: Gaston Wiet, "La Grande Peste Noire en Syrie et en Egypt," *Études d'Orientalisme dédiées à la memoire de Lévi Provençal,* 2 vols. (Paris: G.-P. Maisonneuve et Larose, 1962), 1:381–83.